D0177540

992653553 4

# THE BEAUTIFUL LIFE

# BY THE SAME AUTHOR

*Forsaking the Family*

*Origins*

*The Learning of Love*

*One-Minute Mystic*

*Desert Child*

*Desert Ascent*

*Desert Depths*

# THE BEAUTIFUL LIFE

## TEN NEW COMMANDMENTS:
## BECAUSE LIFE COULD BE BETTER

### SIMON PARKE

BLOOMSBURY

First published in Great Britain 2007

Copyright © 2007 by Simon Parke

The moral right of the author has been asserted

No part of this book may be used or reproduced in any
manner whatsoever without written permission from the
Publisher except in the case of brief quotations
embodied in critical articles or reviews

Bloomsbury Publishing Plc,
36 Soho Square,
London W1D 3QY

Bloomsbury Publishing, London, New York, Berlin

A CIP catalogue record for this book
is available from the British Library

ISBN 978 0 7475 8364 6

10 9 8 7 6 5 4 3 2 1

Typeset by Palimpsest Book Production Limited, Stirlingshire
Printed and bound in Great Britain by Clays Ltd, St Ives plc

The paper this book is printed on is certified by the © 1996
Forest Stewardship Council A.C. (FSC). It is ancient-forest
friendly. The printer holds FSC chain of custody SGS-COC-2061

# ACKNOWLEDGEMENTS

I thank all my teachers,
on whose broad shoulders I sit.
From the twentieth century, I owe the most
perhaps to
Maurice Nicol, A.H. Almaas and Jacob
Needleman.
Thank you.

I thank also my two editors at Bloomsbury,
Rosemary Davidson and Mike Jones,
who made things change,
made things better,
and made things happen; and Mary Tomlinson
is a severe blessing to any text.

I thank Richard Addis,
a very particular angel to me.
Both gracious enough and foolish enough
to believe early in this faltering possibility,
he risked himself freely on its behalf.
Without him, nothing.

To Shellie

*Every night and every day, black Pluto's door stands open wide, but to retrace your steps, and return to the upper air – that is the task, that is the work.*

The Prophetess to Aeneas before his terrifying descent into the underworld.

# CONTENTS

# CONTENTS

# CONTENTS

# A Reading Suggestion

When an asterisk appears in the text, it is an invitation to pause. It is marking a small ending, before another beginning. Sometimes you may want to stay with the ending, before moving on to the beginning.

Something ending is not generally as exciting as something beginning. But it is as necessary for life.

One of the reasons why life is so unhappy is that many of us have lost, or never found, the habit of reflecting on the day, of replaying the day lived through our body. There is a reason for this, and the reason is lack of education. No one ever taught us to listen back to the day. No one ever thought it important enough to take us aside and suggest we gently think about all that has been, both that which gave us heart and that which wounded us, that which lifted us and that which deflated us.

Such details of our day tell us much about ourselves, about how and who we are. But, being poorly educated, we were never told, and now find it hard to listen to such things.

Each day, therefore, we miss the kind instruction of feelings remembered, and thereby abort the possibility for growth. For they would tell us everything we need to know about ourselves. It is the simple and familiar things we need to see, but they are strangely hidden from us.

We fear to pause. For reasons known only to ourselves, we prefer amnesia. And this is sad. For by missing the present reality, we deny ourselves any future.

It needn't be so. We can start by stopping – stopping at the asterisk.

# PRELIMINARIES

This book is primarily concerned with offering ten new commandments or ten skilful attitudes towards the development of a beautiful life. Before reaching them, however, we will take three preliminary steps, for, as painters know, it's all in the preparation.

# STEP ONE

# What This Is, and What This Is Not

*The business of the novelist is to show the sorryness underlying the grandest of things, and the grandeur underlying the sorriest of things.*

Thomas Hardy

A woman once had a dream. She dreamt she was a fire – a blazing fire, full of colour and life. She was a fire woman. And then suddenly, against her will, she finds forming around her a thick crust of lava. It begins to choke and smother the fire. It begins to stifle the life that is her.

And now in the dream, the woman is outside her body of fire, beating at the crust, trying to break it, to loosen its claustrophobic grip, to give the fire inside a chance to breathe, the fire once so bright and vivid.

But she beats in vain. For as her arms begin to ache

and tire, the crust thickens, and soon the air-starved fire is extinguished. The woman is extinguished. In her dream, the life in her is extinguished.

*

A few days later, this woman began to suffer from acute schizophrenia, and her dream became reality. First she felt herself being overcome by a rigid crust. Then she found herself trying to defend herself against this choking death. Finally, she felt herself being extinguished, both spiritually and mentally.

Now, some years later, she still talks of herself as a burnt-out crater, lying in a dark place, only half alive.

*

This is a story of a struggle at the core of a human being, a story of living death. It is the experience of a terrible split in the human psyche and a splintering of identity. The victim knows only desolation, and the loneliness of someone far from where they want to be.

The lava crust can take hold in more routine ways. Sometimes, it is merely the role people play in life, and it can happen without us knowing.

A trumpet on which only military tunes are played might imagine itself to be a military instrument, just as someone who has driven trains for twenty years might imgine themselves a train driver. But neither of these imaginings is so. The trumpet is not a military instrument and the man was not a train driver.

Whatever we do in life, we do it to the best of our ability, for all work is important, but we need never identify ourselves with it. If we do, a phoney definition of ourselves crystallises inside us, and a crust is formed. We become separate from who we are, disconnected.

And when we become disconnected from who we are, however it has happened, it is a long journey home.

What follows is a consideration of that journey – the journey home to a beautiful life.

\*

This is not a self-help book, however. Self-help books are those in which reasonable things are said about your condition, encouraging noises made, manageable targets set, and instant results confidently guaranteed.

This is not so here, for we are neither interested in things instant nor in results. There is nothing wrong with instant in itself. Instant can be good. But as a rule of thumb, if it is instant, it probably doesn't matter very much. Rome was not built in a day. The ocean liner cannot turn on a sixpence. And the human being is both bigger and more complex than both.

There's nothing wrong with results either. Results can be good. But they are never a promise, and never the reason for proceeding. In a society that worships the god of immediate and demonstrable outcomes, results have iconic status. But to seek results above all else is to step on a treadmill of insecure and misplaced striving, in which contortions are more evident than health. You are worth more than that. There are things you can work towards, but nothing you need strive for.

Nothing truly valuable can ever be made into a target.

Instead, we will contemplate only the familiar and simple. The familiar and simple is often hidden from us, covered by a thick cloak of non-seeing. But if we lift the cloak, we will find it reveals much. It is the search that is our responsibility, not the outcome. The journey to the shrine is the shrine itself.

In the meantime, results can take care of themselves.

*

It is not therefore a book full of guidelines or advice. This is not done maliciously. I simply don't know what you should do. Our journeys are different. What particular suggestions would a woman hang-gliding over the Pyrenees have for the motorist slowly making his way through downtown Bangkok? They are both journeys, but that is about their only similarity. Your path to freedom will look very different from mine.

Existence is not black and white.
Existence is interconnected paths of infinite variety,
And the world a most various place.
As travellers we can walk only a few paths.
And meet only a few travellers.
There is a home place.
But the journey for each traveller is unique.

No wonder teachers from the East refused both to write and speak, opting only to point. Words from the mouth of another would have been an insult to the uniqueness of their pupils. It was their personal journey, after all. What had the teacher's words got to do with it?

*

It is not an academic book, either. Academic books tend to work on the principle that thought is all we have, that when we reach the end of thought we have said everything that can sensibly be said.

This book has a different assumption. Thought is a marvellous and remarkable tool, and can lead us to the threshold of some extraordinary views. But to visit the places themselves we need to go beyond thought. Thought can show – but cannot transport or transform.

The assumption from here on is that all important truth lies beyond the mental struggle. Some may say that means stepping into the territory of value judgements, and unverifiable fantasy. I would say in reply that there is not a human being on earth who has not always lived in that territory. Our intellectual life is based on little more than chance associations in our past, which over time have become more or less fixed. There is little thought that is free, and no clean knowledge – only interpreted knowledge.

We all live in a fantasy world – the only question is whether one fantasy is more truthful than another.

So perhaps we must call this a spiritual book, and read it as such. A spiritual book is one that is happy to remain open-ended. It desires to engage, but not to convince. Reading it will be like watching smoke from an extinguished candle, fluid and smooth in the air, before it dissipates gradually into the big space. We do not argue with the smoke – we merely contemplate it. It has no claim on us but the attention we give it. The smoke does not prove anything, but suggests many things. It does not make sense – but might make things clear.

To say that it is a spiritual book, however, is not to suggest that it should be your friend. The aim of a spiritual book is to stimulate life – not explain it. A spiritual book can hardly contain its passion for *you* – but it is less caring of your *feelings*. Indeed, on occasions, a spiritual book can feel less like self-help and more like self-destruction. During your relationship with such a book, therefore, it should probably be thrown across the floor in anger, stamped on several times in frustration, left to rot on the sideboard for a while, held still in an occasional moment of revelation – and retrieved from the bin at least twice.

But no one can point you to anything you do not already know. You alone are the alchemist of your humanity. The power is given to you alone to turn base metal into gold, to turn such base energies as fear, worry, anger, deceit, hatred, and delusion into generosity, openness, spontaneity, kindness, courage and awareness.

This is your genius, and it would not be a spiritual book if it did not start with your genius.

And genius can go a long way by first noticing simple and familiar things: both the sorryness and the grandeur.

*

We started with the story of the woman's dream, because it contains as accurate a picture of the human race as has ever been portrayed. Cut off from who we truly are, we become a stranger not only to ourselves but in the world, and to others.

In this desperate situation, our only security lies in the conviction that we are in control. This is what we cling to. Living outside our true nature, we cease to *trust* life, and try instead to *control* it. Unable to trust, we must manipulate our way forward.

In the pages that follow, we shall never be far from

the story of the fire woman, excluded from herself. It is a story that aches for redemption, for healing and for homecoming.

Perhaps she shall experience homecoming. These things are not impossible.

*If a friend today were to point me towards a truth, where would they be pointing?*

# STEP TWO

# On Discerning Truth

*Advice to the mushroom picker: 'Stay away from those surrounded by dead flies.'*

*Anon*

When two people meet for the first time, they are each feeling their way towards the being of the other. In the early exchanges, though it is opinions that are shared, it is not the opinions of the other that they seek. The more pressing question is: Who are they? It is not their achievements we want to discover, but their nature.

They may talk of shoe shops, foreign affairs or Dalmatians, but such matters are not the pressing concern. When two people meet for the first time, somewhere deep within each they are both silently asking the same question: What comprises this life I have just met? Will I like it or hate it? Is it twisted or beautiful? What is the truth of this person?

It is the purpose of this book to consider the truth of people and the truthful possibilities within them. We will reflect on both the unhelpful activities that damage, and the skilful attitudes that nurture.

*

From here on, therefore, the concepts of good and bad will always be secondary to true and false. The human journey is primarily about becoming true, rather than good. Truth is primary to goodness, because without truth goodness can have no sense of what it is. Goodness imagined by the false is sometimes a most terrible thing. Hitler believed he was good to be saving Germany from Jews, gypsies and homosexuals. Many others thought him good too.

It is more important to be true than good.

*

In pursuit of truth, we will look always with the inner eye. We are not concerned here with external things, things seen and reported. Rather, we are concerned with the internal textures out of which we create our lives. We are concerned with the energies that comprise us, rather than the rules imposed on us.

Other people's rules are mere expressions of their egos. They have nothing to do with us. The awake do not need rules, for they spontaneously create appropriate ways as the setting demands.

We are human beings rather than human doings. What we are must always come before what we do, for how we are defines our world. If we are negative within, we will take in negative impressions, like someone breathing in exhaust fumes.

Consider the one who allows ninety-nine pieces of praise to pass them by, hearing only the one slight criticism, and taking huge offence.

And then consider the one who sings even when they are losing, in pleasure at the other's excitement at winning. They are losing happily.

Our real life is not outer events but inner states. How we are defines our world.

In what follows, what you do is almost irrelevant. It is why you do things that reveals all.

*

This sort of truth is not a subject taught in our schools. Discerning truth may be the greatest challenge we face on earth, but it is not in the curriculum, not part of our education. After all, it is neither academic discipline nor vocational training, so what place could it have? And anyway, it's the sort of thing you pick up as you go along, isn't it?

Not so.

We do not pick it up, and the passing years in them-selves teach us little. The consequences of this are most hurtful, both for us and for those with whom we share the planet.

We learn many things in life, certainly, and some of them are remarkably complex and clever, but they are all utterly useless, until we know what it is to be human. Until such time, we are the famous bull in the china shop – temperamentally unsuited to our surroundings, unaware of the power in our hands, and destroying every-thing we touch.

True education is our undoing. For true education is undoing all the conditioning that has denied us the beauty and happiness of living.

*

What follows is an ancient and simple teaching, though not an easy one. Its outlines are there in many centuries, settings, cultures and religions.

Only one thing is ever required of us – that we give up everything we imagine we know. From here on, all assumed knowledge counts for nothing. Once we give up everything we imagine we know, our progress towards truth becomes a good deal freer, and life more hopeful.

Nan-in receives a university professor who has come to enquire about Zen. Nan-in serves tea. He fills his cup, as a good host might. But he carries on pouring until the cup is spilling over.

The university professor watches until he can contain himself no longer.

'It is over-full!' he says. 'No more will go in!'

'Like this cup,' replies Nan-in, 'you are full of your speculations and opinions. How can I show you Zen unless you first empty your cup?'

\*

Along the way, therefore, there may need to be some unlearning of old things, and some removal of old clothes. There may need to be a dismantling of things certain, an unknotting of the mind, some loss of control and some duties abandoned. We can allow madness; we can allow the heart to be washed in sadness. There may need to be some failures re-named, and all things reviewed.

Such things are wonderful, for there are no eggs in last year's nest.

\*

Whether we will permit ourselves the possibility of truth is open to question. For many, truth is something no longer worth searching for. They have become disillusioned by, and even angry with, such talk. Truth is dismissed as merely the story on top, the one told by those currently in power.

There is validity in such disillusionment. History tends to be written by the victors on their own behalf, while the present is dominated by the stupidly convinced, who use their convictions to dominate and control.

What price truth therefore?

*

Truth in this book refers to psychological truth, the truth of people, which is entirely observable. The setting for psychological truth is a connected universe of cause and effect, in which one thing leads to another, where outcomes have origins.

Let us take a simple example. The child of a depressed mother will struggle with self-esteem throughout its life. This will be the outcome of this particular origin – poor stimulation when the social brain of the child was forming. The child got used to a lack of concern for its well-being, and expects nothing more thereafter.

Or again, see the child who grows up refusing to allow anger against its parent. The anger they feel inside is reckoned by them to be unacceptable, and is therefore denied. Such people will be those who forever feel guilty. They will turn the unexpressed anger in on themselves, and experience feelings of guilt. A pattern of guilt in a life is almost always the result of repressed anger. Psychological outcomes have psychological origins.

The authenticity of psychological truth is clearly

established by observation of the world, and even more powerfully through self-observation. Buddha based all things on such truth. Not for him grand truth from the skies, imposed on us from the outside, and to be taken on trust. He believed only in the truth he could observe within himself. It became in time a clear window on the world.

It is such truth we consider here.

*

The hidden history of our childhood commits us to patterns that are entirely predictable, for we live in a universe where outcomes have origins. There is nothing random about our personality. Our personality is formed in response to life. We each live our histories as best we can.

And so it is that some are left feeling they must succeed at all costs, driven to do and achieve; and some are left with a black hole of abandonment within, which they feel no one can embrace or fill; some lock themselves in an emotional castle tower, carefully observing all who approach; whilst others are stubborn in poor self-esteem, down on themselves but craving attention.

As we have noted, some live crippled by guilt, judging themselves and others, and some seek authority behind which to hide, untrusting of themselves; while others are restless in search of ever-fresh options, desperately riding each tide of escape and thrill. Some live the compulsive concern of the determined saviour, needing to be needed; while others take the world on in bullish aggression, at home only with confrontation.

These familiar outcomes have origins. Psychological truth is as observable and enlightening as the sun rising in the morning.

When we prepare for truth, it is for psychological truth.

*

Certain things *have* changed down the centuries.

We don't now imagine that our leaders will tell us the truth – for power does not encourage it. They have more money than us and a larger staff – but perhaps no more wisdom. We are a cynical generation, who expect only the crooked or the vain to make it to the top. Certainly we do not expect to find truth-tellers there.

Neither are we persuaded by mass appeal. Some of the most absurd and dangerous movements in history have been widely applauded and adored. Many still are.

Hitler drew ecstatic and committed crowds. Like many leaders, he was an extremely successful communicator. He motivated many, with poor self-image and an unhappy history, to believe they could succeed, believe they were part of something big and glorious. 'Believe the new truth and all things are possible,' he said. And so, together, leader and followers walked confidently into the abyss.

*

I remember only one key fact from my education, and it was written on the toilet wall: 'Eat shit: four million flies can't be wrong.'

The prophet had spoken, and it was the one lesson I took with me into adulthood. Just because everyone imagines it is so does not mean that it is so, for everyone is stupid. It was written not in gold lettering like the school motto in the big hall, but in weak and scrawled black biro, in a hidden-away place.

But it was the biro, and not the gold, that held truth.

*

Political success, therefore, is unlikely to be one of the truth-teller's credentials, for people do not vote for truth. They want acceptable lies. If you want to be successful, don't tell the truth.

Buddha, Socrates and Jesus all died rather lonely deaths. Each was an idiot in the original Greek meaning of the word – 'a private person, one who possessed something'. They were sufficient in themselves, but lonely in the world. A good-sized majority voted for the death of Socrates. Buddha's followers vainly tried to have him die in a place other than Kusinara, which was a dreary little town, a jungle outpost of mud walls, and a backwater of civilisation. They would have preferred one of the big cities for his send-off. While there were only four standing at the foot of the cross on which Jesus died, and one of those was his mother.

Every country, religion or organisation tends to get the leader it deserves: the leader who addresses them on their level, however low that may be, and who is able to make their darkness look like light. We create structures in which only liars and dissemblers can thrive; we choose the clever over the wise; and then entertain ourselves by exposing them for what they always were. People like us.

We call this sophistication.

*

Truth-tellers tend to be reluctant public figures, as they have no need or desire to display themselves. Wisdom does not want to see itself in lights. It wishes to enlighten others.

Socrates and Hippias were a case in point. Socrates was very critical of people like Hippias who discovered that 'wisdom' could bring fame and fortune. Socrates said that the wise of earlier times had not been wealthy public figures; they had been 'too simple to notice the value of money'. Hippias missed Socrates' irony, and heard that as a criticism of the wise of earlier times. Hippias saw such people as poor naïve fools, who had missed a trick. But he didn't. He made a fortune from wisdom.

But for Plato's writings, Socrates' life would be little known now. He was shy of the limelight, but has turned out to be greatly remembered. Hippias, on the other hand, who sought out fame, is now forgotten.

*

But whether truth-tellers are public or private figures, how might we recognise them? What characteristics will give them away as authentic? If a 'truth-teller' post were created, and interviews arranged, what would we want on the specification for candidates?

If I was on the panel drawing up a shortlist for our imaginary – and unlikely – post, I might have scribbled at the top of my page the words 'Suffering', 'Judge', 'Homesick', 'Vision', and 'Nonsense'.

1) Suffering: I would be interested to know what the candidate had done with their suffering. Had they acknowledged the presence of pain in their past, and understood its legacy in their life? We hurt people out of our unexamined suffering. There is no tyrant with a happy childhood; no ethnic cleansing arising out of experiences of joy and trust. Once given power, the tyrant merely recreates at a national level the terrors of their family past.

This is significant because most tyranny we endure is rather more routine. The woman who returns home in a bad mood and makes everyone's life hell for half an hour is a victim passing on her own unexamined suffering to others. It may be small-scale tyranny but it is most unpleasant.

Truth-tellers will need to have befriended their personal sadness. We hurt each other when we live and speak from a place of unacknowledged pain. The truth cannot come from a place such as this.

2) Judge: I would be interested to know whether the individual had a judgemental disposition. Do people blossom in the hopeful and peaceful presence of the candidate? Or do they wither in either spoken or unspoken criticism?

Someone living the beautiful life creates beautiful situations without speaking. Their work is done almost before they open their mouths. They create virtue around them by being, not telling.

A judgemental disposition, on the other hand, is the property of a damaged and negative soul, which can create fear, but not virtue.

The truth-teller will be aware of their own deep incompleteness, or as Jesus put it, aware of the beam in their eye. With a beam in your eye, you can barely see others, let alone judge them.

3) Homesick: The successful candidate should make listeners homesick. The best art, philosophy and religion is concerned with a strange longing for home. It is as if we do not quite feel at home where we are, as though we wander through an empty house, pushing a door here, banging at a wall there, shouting out occasionally, wondering if this is in fact home, and where we are meant to be – or just a passing-through place?

We suppress this longing, however, for it is too painful. We become busy with doing instead. We make the best of the incomplete, and label all else as unobtainable.

The truth-teller, however, will bring this ache for homecoming painfully to the surface. The truth-teller will remind us of the original figure of flame, now smothered. The truth-teller has no wish to construct something new. Merely to help us to recover that which we've lost.

4) Vision: What does it look like?

True vision does three things: It sees things as they are, the sorryness and the grandeur; it connects people to each other, in both curiosity and solidarity; and arises from pure will, a strong and unpolluted river within.

The truth-teller's vision will arise from their being. People can only create around them what they themselves are.

27

5) Nonsense: The truth-teller will know that their words are nonsense. The truth-teller will know that all words are a collapsing staircase, a vanity of inaccuracy. Truth cannot be explained or told. It cannot live in formulations – merely noticed in passing and greeted with a smile. Truth must show itself, manifest itself, in ways and means unbiddable and mysterious. The truth-teller will not want anything built on their words, but hopes only that life will grow in the gaps in between.

We must now just hope for some applicants.

*Today, I will asterisk my day. I will be one who pauses at possible moments. I will listen for how people's comments make me feel, for it is rare that I am completely neutral about remarks made. I will listen also for the roots of my own comments. I will listen not only to what I say, but the spirit in which I say it. I will not judge anyone else or myself. Just contemplate the event, allow it to speak, and follow each golden thread my listening presents.*

*We will seek the truth.*

# STEP THREE

# Sleep, Law, and a Glossary

*A time is coming when people will go mad, and when they meet someone who is not mad, they will turn to him and say, 'You are out of your mind,' just because he is not like them.*

Abbot Anthony, *fourth century* AD

If one night we see someone sleepwalking towards us, we might gently try to wake them up, or at least guide them back to their bed where they can do no harm to themselves. They may have guided themselves skilfully thus far, but it is a limited venture, and one which is literally best put to bed.

What we don't do, however, is put the one sleep-walking in charge of the nation's nuclear arsenal, nor do we ask them to advise us on religion, law, health and education, nor would we insist that they are just the one to sort out our family problems, or tell us what to do about death and suffering, or write a comment column in a national paper, or become Prime Minister. They are asleep after all, not conscious to reality. What would they know about anything?

Yet Eastern philosophy would say that this description of the sleepwalker describes us all. The suggestion is that we are so cut off from reality, glimpsing only tiny aspects of it, that we are best described as asleep – both to ourselves and the world. We impersonate consciousness as a sleepwalker impersonates watchfulness. But neither is the real thing.

So the one with his hands on the nuclear arsenal is asleep; those guiding our religions, law, health and education are asleep; those bringing up families are asleep; those speaking about death and suffering are asleep. The sharp-tongued comment-columnist is asleep. Those running the country are asleep. Those telling us to wake up are asleep. We are drugged by illusion, blind to reality, ignorant of who we are.

We are the living dead, pretending life.

There is madness in such talk, but is there not at least a trace of something in this diagnosis to which we can relate? For good or ill, we do appear to be trapped inside an existence someone else has made, reacting in ways we do not always understand.

*

So who or what has created us? And if we are trapped in an unnatural or contrived vision, just where will fresh and authentic vision come from? How can something finite such as ourselves see outside itself to repair the damage done? You might as well ask rock to think beyond the mountain. It only knows the mountain. So how can it think beyond it?

This is the problem. To see beyond our minds we would have to cut our heads off and take leave of our minds. Yet when people do take leave of their minds on earth they are usually considered to be crazy.

Waking up is not a matter of thought, however, but of will. Some are woken by anguish, and some by wonder, but if we do not will it, it will not happen. We will be as those who are always thinking of leaving their job, always talking about it, threatening it, dreaming of it – but never actually going.

Such people do not leave because, ultimately, they do not will it.

At the end it will have been our will and not our thought that has shaped our lives. Our thinking entertains, but our will determines. And history shows there are many who do not will their own waking.

*

History also demonstrates the inability of external laws to change anyone or solve anything. Fine ideas and noble calls have been shown not to work. Moral exhortations to live better lives are always applauded from afar, but ignored within. We put statuettes of our spiritual or political teachers on our sideboards, or pictures of them on our wall, or their books by our bed – and then live the life we want to live.

Or more accurately, the life our compulsions lead us to live.

There are not many certainties in life but perhaps this is one: people do what they want to do. People do what they want to do, and everything and everyone else, including their particular gurus, must fit around this central project of self-centred action.

Maturity is acquiring a more spontaneous life, one free from the constricting wants of self. But external commands full of 'shoulds' and 'oughts' do not take us there.

*

The weight of accumulated evidence is heavy. Beautiful ideals do not penetrate the human heart from the outside. How could it be otherwise? We simply have no place within us to receive and nurture them.

It is like trying to remember a sentence from a foreign language. We have no place where these new words can be kept. It is the same with other people's commands. Someone may command me to be generous with my money, and I would like to be, but I am too mean, and the command does not change that, nor will it ever. Instead, I will just feel bad that I am mean, and from now on try to pretend otherwise.

This is what happens when external morals are placed on us.

External law will fail until it becomes internal law. Telling humans what to do is like asking stones to flow. Stones cannot flow until they become fluid within. And so it is with the human. It is not worth anyone telling you what to do, because you will do what you are.

External law tells you what to do.
Internal law reveals how to be.
In this book, we are concerned with internal law.

Little wonder that Jesus reduced the famous Ten Commandments to two. He asked only that his followers love God and love their neighbour. It is a refreshing and bold return to the spirit behind the original ten. But they are still demanding requirements for the confused human animal, who experiences only occasional and brief bursts of moral energy.

It is our being which must come first.

\*

What follows is my definition of some of the key characters we meet on the beautiful journey.

## PERSONALITY

Personality is the outer reach of our psychology. It is how people know us, and perhaps how we know ourselves. But it is not who we are. 'Persona' originally meant 'mask'.

Personality is the early adjustment of our true selves into something less true. It is inevitable in human life, but not something defining. The development of our personality was crucial for survival in the early years of existence, but now limits us. It is not worthy of us. To condemn our true self to live through our personality is to stable a magnificent horse in a cardboard box.

If we define ourselves by our personality, we are defining ourselves by a lie.

We are vulnerable at birth, open to things, trusting of people and circumstances, in awe of the mystery, and absorbent of each discovery. We imagine that this new kingdom is like the marvellous world of the womb, only better. Just as safe, but more exciting. But it isn't so, and the shock is savage. The trust we learnt in the womb has to be unlearnt, as animal instincts of survival take over. From here on, we need to look after number one. And number one is ourselves.

And so the soft and receptive original us, hardens and becomes resistant; the trusting part of us becomes separate and suspicious, and the open part of us closed. From feeling at one with all things we become at one only with ourselves, and begin to define ourselves externally by our physical bodies; and internally, by the thoughts and feelings that pass through our psyches like screeching monkeys swinging their way through the jungle.

The outcome is what we call our personality. And we take this personality increasingly seriously.

See the child who is never the centre of attention, and feels unbearable rejection. They discover that when they are ill they receive attention, and even people's good wishes. From here on, being ill becomes an important part of their life, as the search for consolation continues into adulthood. A disposition towards sickness becomes part of their self-understanding. Yet it is a contrivance, and nothing to do with who they truly are.

*

Our personality is not who we are. Neither is it who we were, or who we will be. Essentially, we are that open, trusting, absorbent, and awed character who entered the world so full of hope, before circumstances forced change upon us. We were the fire in our starting story, before we became hardened to life, and died.

We understand why it was so. Only now we would like to return home. We would like to smash the crust and reawaken the fire. Our personality formed to protect us from the terror of life, but now has become the terror itself.

Our personality is our self-image pretending to be us.

We are like actors rehearsing a play. In the early days, we laugh about our parts, but then, as time goes on, come gradually to believe our parts to be the truth about who we are. Suddenly, it is no longer a play rehearsal. This is for real. So the one playing the villain actually believes he is the villain; the one playing the jolly character actually believes she is jolly; and likewise for the depressed man, the moral teacher, the misunderstood woman, the gung-ho adventurer, the wise old head, the helpful friend, the angry leader, the frightened teenager, and so on.

No wonder we feel without substance sometimes, without foundations. We are living in a construction that should have been demolished years ago. The human personality is a hostel to pass through, not a home to live in. The human personality, whether attractive or fractured, cheerful or withdrawn, determined or cautious, is nothing more than a compelling illusion. To that extent, we could be said to live in a tomb.

In order to come home, we will need to get beyond our personality. As was written a long time ago, 'The torn-off mask lays bare the thing that is.'[1]

## EGO

I imagine ego as the figure who sits on the throne of your personality. It rules your personality as one who

[1] Lucretius.

rules a kingdom, and like all rulers, it does not like its kingdom to be threatened.

We live in a world charged with anger, fear and worry, and ruthless in the pursuit of personal worth. This is the territory of the ego. Ego is the systematic affirmation of both our emotional reactions and our stampede towards individual value. It both supports and applauds the surging energies of feelings that run through us. It makes us believe that they are us, who we are.

Until someone has begun to free themselves from this grip, there are no possibilities, for there are no possibilities in untruth.

Ego, as it is, has no interest in your well-being. Indeed, it has great interest in your psychological demise. The only interest it has in keeping you alive is keeping itself alive, for it dies with your physical death. It has no eternity – just manipulation. Everything it will whisper in your ear is a lie. It will do anything, and sacrifice anything, in order to survive. It will make you feel angry, bored, frustrated, judgemental, irritated, superior, whatever it takes – anything to distract you from what will awaken truth in you.

We will not declare war on the ego, however, for existence is one and all things related. To declare war on our ego would be to declare war on ourselves. Nothing in the world is single. All things abhorrent relate closely to all things good.

Instead, we will be content simply to note our ego,

and understand it. Insecure and frightened, it will keep appearing in different forms, long after we imagine it gone. And when it does, we will simply note it again. Like a naughty child, it is less damaging for being watched; and more whole for being allowed.

## ESSENCE

Essence is our innermost psychology, and distinct from our personality. Essence is our essential nature, our truest identity. The seven wonders of the world become an irrelevance in comparison to one's experience of this phenomenon. Tradition describes this self within the heart of us as more radiant than the sun, purer than the snow, and subtler than ether.

It is indestructible, available and your truest self. From here on, when I speak of essence, I speak of the truest you.

Essence is the truth about yourself.
Personality, the untruth told to yourself and others.
Essence's truth exists irrespective of time or setting.
Personality's untruth is moulded by childish needs,
    cultural expectations and the opinions of others.
Our essence is a prowling lion, all powerful
    possibility.
Our personality is a scavenger, living off the scraps.

## THE SOUL

The soul lives and mediates between our personality and our essence. It is the grand field of all our operations, and the creator of our individual worlds. It is the place within you that receives impressions, the place that holds experiences, and determines responses. A human soul is variable in size – it can be larger than the world, and it can be smaller than a pea. It is ever-changing, ever-responding to the psychic chemistry of the moment, and crucial to our story.

Our soul receives its character from its relationship to our personality and our essence.

*

This book is for those who sense there is a journey to be had. It is an exploration beyond what appears inevitably so, beyond our mechanical lives of predictable reaction.

In the making of this journey, some things will not matter. Your colour, creed, gender, sexuality, culture, social status, or ethnic origin are of no more significance here than your shoe size or telephone number. The only assumption I make is that you are human, for it is human beauty that we attempt to explore. Only humans can reflect on the nature of the machine their souls inhabit, and that is all that will be asked of you.

I will not ask you to believe words. I will not ask you to believe promises. And I will ask you only to believe your feelings in as much as they lead you back to their origins in your past – for you did not have your present feelings at birth. Feelings are clues that lead us to treasure. They are not the treasure themselves.

You will take nothing on trust. But you might occasionally take a risk as the journey proceeds. Thomas, a doubting member of Jesus' following, surprisingly risked placing his hand in the wounds of Jesus' crucified body, in order to test out a theory he found hard to believe.

*

A man had been searching for the truth all his life, but now he was getting old, and feared he would never find it. Then he was told of a wise teacher, and he decided to seek him out. This could be his last chance. When the teacher saw him approaching, he came out to greet him. 'Leave your followers and your baggage at the door, and come inside,' he said. The man was a bit surprised to hear this, as he had no followers and no baggage, but he understood what the teacher meant, so he did as he was told, left his followers and baggage outside, went in, and discovered the truth.

Sometimes, to discover new things, we have to leave everything we think we know outside. Everything.

*Today, I will place a spy in my machine body. The spy will report back to me machine-like activity on my part, automatic action or reaction, whether emotional or physical. The spy will remark on anything that is predictable, repeated patterns of behaviour, anything that is not spontaneous. From the reports of this spy, this other me, this quiet observer, I will build up a dossier revealing the answer to the question: Who lives who? Do I live my machine, or does my machine live me?*

# TEN NEW COMMANDMENTS FOR THE LONG JOURNEY HOME

# 1

# Be Present

*Yesterday's an illness, and tomorrow's a disease.*

*Anon*

A man in a village lost his horse one night when it broke out of the enclosure and disappeared into the hills. The other villagers saw what a disaster this could be, and commiserated with him. 'Terrible news about the horse,' they said. 'Could be bad news, could be good news,' he replied, standing firmly in the present.

A week later his lost horse returned, with twenty wild horses. Suddenly the man had twenty-one horses! The other villagers were ecstatic for him, seeing what this could mean. 'Brilliant news about the horses!' they said. 'Could be good news, could be bad news,' he replied, standing firmly in the present.

It wasn't long before he was taming them, but one particularly wild horse threw him off, breaking his leg. The villagers were distraught because they could see what this might mean. 'Terrible news about your leg,' they said. 'Could be bad news, could be good news,' he replied, standing firmly in the present.

Two weeks later, the country went to war, and the recruiting sergeants came to the village to enlist the men. But because our man had a broken leg, he was spared the call-up. The other villagers were delighted for him, seeing what this could mean. 'Marvellous news about you staying safe in the village!' they said. 'Could be good news, could be bad news,' he replied, standing firmly in the present.

\*

The past is stale. The future does not exist. The present is fresh. Everything but the present is an illusion, and we need a very good reason to choose not to be there. The past is stale bread. The future is no bread. The present is fresh bread. I know which I am opting for.

\*

The invitation to 'be present' does not initially appear challenging. After all, where else could we be? To imagine we could be anywhere else is laughable, nonsense.

48

But we should not be fooled. This is not nonsense. Few of us do live in the present.

I well remember a sign outside a house. *Beware of the cat.* My friend and I laughed when we saw it, amusing ourselves at the idea of being afraid of a cat. Until, that is, we met the cat. Then we stopped laughing, stepping back in fear, and understanding the sign at last. When it said: *Beware of the cat*, it was being serious.

Equally, this first commandment is serious, in that being present is simply one of the most transforming of human acts. The present is the only real life. All else is false. As we have said, the past is stale and the future does not exist.

Those who can think only of times past will spend their life in mourning. Those who can think only of the bus as they stand at the bus stop will spend all their life waiting.

This moment you are living is not an interval between appointments. It is the appointment. There is only the present. But to be present is not simple.

\*

Being present is an inner act, as all significant acts are. And it is the act of being present to the moment, as opposed to being present somewhere else.

Because so little of us is present, we struggle to see things as they are. We are a personality splintered by

49

past and future, without the ability to perceive things truly. We are a diaspora, a people once close, now scattered round the world, and with different concerns.

Being present cuts through past entanglements and future anxieties, like a blade through ice. It brings you together. And it is the realisation that all is quite perfect.

\*

Ask a pig what it will be doing next year, and it will look at you blankly, and be perhaps a little dumbfounded. This is not only because it can't understand what you are saying, but also because it is such a stupid question. For the pig next year does not exist. There is only now – the mud, the sun, the potato peelings and the farmer scratching its back.

Yet somehow, and for some reason, we always prefer to be somewhere other than the present. It is like visiting an unpopular aunt: we always manage to find excuses not to do it. We slope off instead, either to the past or the future, apparently unruffled by the fact that neither of them exists.

The past has been pensioned off, whilst the future is not even at the ideas stage. And given their non-existence, it will not come as a surprise to learn that every moment we spend in either of those places is a moment utterly wasted, and one that cannot be clawed back. It is on a par with being given one million pounds in crisp clean notes, and throwing them in the sea. It is a large gift thrown away, and the end of the only possibility on offer.

There is only the present.

*

There is an old saying that if you do not seize the moment then someone else will. It is not only an old saying, but also a true one. And for some of us, that thieving someone will be our past. Our past can cast a very long shadow across our lives, and deny us much. Some never get clear of the shadow, remaining unable to live in the present, and therefore unable to live freely and spontaneously in the world. This is sad.

For all of us, to some degree or other, the past is internalised in the very structure of our body, in the way we think, feel and move. We have absorbed and absorbed and absorbed and are now so weighed down by our personal history, much of it unexamined and unknown, that we wouldn't know where our past ends and we begin.

Most never get beyond the child in them, for most do not stop to ask what pain the child felt. They have the appearance of adults, but live as the hidden child. Had they dared ask what pain the child felt, so much would have become apparent, so much would have become clear, so much would have become free and laughing and fearless. But most do not listen to that child. They fear the answer and, more particularly, the feelings the answer might stir up. There is no growth without feeling, no growth without the painful unfreezing of the past.

*

We each have a past. Our past has been overwhelmingly influential. But let us be clear here: we are not our past. We are our present. The past might have made us, but it does not define us. That's just the ego talking. And you will remember from our introduction that the ego is a compulsive liar. Your ego wants you lost in your past, for in your past is much scaffolding across which it can scuttle like a cockroach, stirring up phoney emotions and reactions. In the present, there is no scaffolding.

Your history has done its work, influencing every decision you make. You hate the hold that history has over you, but strangely, you make no plans to leave. History has made you a prisoner, but you aren't trying to escape. There is a nasty fear inside you, that if you leave the past behind you might actually cease to exist. So you loiter there, whether in subservience or defiance.

The only happy figure in this desperate scene is your ego. It really doesn't mind what you do in your past as long as you stay there, allowing memory to define your every move. As you remain rooted there, your phoney personality feels ever more real, ever more defining of who you are.

But just to irritate the ego, remember: the past might have made us, but it does not define us.

\*

The other non-existent refuge is the future. For some of us, the future is more compelling than the past. We are those who like to move on. The future is the land of opportunity, and we are all for opportunity. We wish to break out and make waves in the big blue beyond. And so we become those who make plans. 'You have to live the dream!' as they say.

But this is not so. That is our ego talking again. To live the dream is a romantic notion, and a foolish one. It makes good movies, but terrible life.

Let any dream you harbour take care of itself, without undue encouragement from you. Instead, go about the simple if demanding business of living the present. The dream you have may well be given to you. They often are, and perhaps in a manner better than you ever dared imagine. But if it is to happen and if it is to be good, it will emerge in its own time, while you seek the only good available – the kingdom presently within, for it is there that reality is changed.

No dream in itself is worth living. There was a woman who had lived in the city all her life, but who dreamt of living in the countryside. The city was where she knew people, but she longed to be elsewhere, somewhere better, in the countryside. She had never lived there, but she knew it was better than where she was. That was her future, no question, and she was impatient and unhappy as she waited.

She did finally make it happen, but was back in the city within eighteen months. It had not been what she expected.

There is only the present, but dreams cannot live there, which is the surest sign that they do not, in themselves, exist. If they do turn out to have substance, it will be as part of something bolder, grander, and much more deserving of wonder than your current hope. But we start by being present.

Truth is always practical and understands that child minders need to be organised, holidays need to be booked, and jokes in crackers need to be written in August. So we do these things. But we do them with an amused smile, as one who knows the future does not exist and can therefore never be truly planned. We then return as soon as we can to the present, where the only reality lies.

*

Your ego will tell you that to live in the present is simply not practical. But it is, and it is worth it. It is like shutting out the noise of a busy road. The silence is deafening. Just for this moment, you are free from the different moods that press their emotional case on your psyche. Just for this moment, the mental tyranny is quiet, for you are in the space between thoughts. You are problem-free. Just for this moment, you are neither battling within nor without, but peaceful in between, free just to be.

Your truest self responds to such space, like a flower responds to sunlight.

*

There is no greater gift to yourself than being in the present. In one sense, it is the only gift that matters. For only in the present are we conscious, awake to the moment, which is why yesterday's an illness and tomorrow's a disease.

This does not mean that you have not lived your past. Your past is rich with significance. But it is a springboard, not a chaperone. Neither does it mean that you do not have a future. Your future is bright without your planning, an unfolding mystery, with many arrivals to enjoy along the way. But an arrival is only worth the journey travelled. If we have not been present to the journey, we can hardly be present to the arrival.

It would be like crossing the finishing line of the marathon without having run the race. It would be an entirely empty experience.

*

The pig knows these things.

The pig knows that tomorrow can be a disease, and yesterday, an illness.

So we let the pig instruct us in the profound things of life. There is the sun, the potato peel, the mud and the farmer scratching its back. Does there need to be anything else?

*

*Today for a moment I will stop my various hallucinations about yesterday, tomorrow or later, and be present to myself: present to the present. I will allow myself to feel the impact of the ordinary, which is in fact deeper than any ocean, and more eternal than the sun. My life thus stopped is my life strangely started. Perhaps I will attempt it more than once today.*

# 2

## Observe Yourself

*The foolish reject what they see, not what
they think. The wise reject what they
think, and not what they see . . . observe
things as they are and don't pay
attention to other people.*

Huang-Po

Al Hallaj, the Sufi saint of tenth-century Persia, was
sentenced to death for heresy, because he had dared to
sing of his identity with God. His skin was slowly stripped
from his body. He was scourged and mutilated, and then
hung on a cross to await his death. His pupils watched,
and then ventured near, to listen for his last words. What
would he say? Would he exhort them to holiness perhaps?
Scream angry abandonment, or call them to forgiveness?

The answer was none of these. This man, who had
taught them so much about God, had just one thing to
say: 'Study yourself.'

\*

The invitation is to observe yourself. It is the invitation to accurate inner seeing, to pay attention to how you are. It's about noticing the simple and familiar and acquiring accurate diagnosis.

When I go to the doctor, I do not want to be drowned in warm concern, but to be given an accurate diagnosis. For without accurate diagnosis there can be no cure. If alongside accurate diagnosis, the doctor turns out to be a warm-hearted individual, then aren't I fortunate? But it isn't essential. I want truth, not chocolates, clarity, not cake.

Only the correct diagnosis is essential. The friendly doctor who gives the wrong diagnosis is a smiling nightmare, as are those who misdiagnose the human soul. Both cause extreme damage and heartache.

The invitation, therefore, is to observe yourself, to live with divided attention. You do what you must do. But you also watch yourself doing what you must do. This means that sometimes you will become that strangest of things – a whistleblower on yourself.

This observing of self is important, for if you don't, who will? No one else can observe you, for no one else knows you.

And you will have time to do this, for you cannot observe anyone else, just as they cannot observe you. To observe anyone else is mental gossip and distraction. Pay no attention to other people.

*

Observe yourself, therefore, but observe yourself gently. Let all observation be gentle and the quality of mercy not strained. For there is nothing in ourselves with which we are at war.

Imagine if I murdered someone. Perhaps I would then drive their body at night to a lake. I would then weigh it down with stones, and throw it into the depths. The body sinks, and the water returns to calm. And as the days, months and years pass, I begin to believe that I have got away with it.

But twenty years later, I am driving alongside that water with my son. My son turns to me and says what a wonderful lake it is. Outwardly I agree. But inwardly I die. For I know what lies beneath the surface.

We die inwardly at everything we cannot bring to the surface. This is why we invite gentle rather than harsh self-observation.

See the figure trying to train a group of young soldiers. They are not doing very well. Everyone is all over the place. Yet somehow the trainer does not seem to mind. He does not shout. He does not coerce. There is no violence in his approach towards this disparate bunch of rookies. If they become obedient, it is because they have chosen it.

59

Compare this figure to another man with some young recruits. He is a shouting, hectoring drill sergeant, who uses fear to create obedience. The rookies do not choose obedience. If they become obedient, it is because it is beaten into them.

One is gentle. One is harsh. We will allow only the gentle within ourselves.

*

Observe yourself. But observe yourself gently. This is the skilful way, for it allows honesty to precede any attempts at purity.

It is something both religion and moralistic societies have always found hard. In such settings, the appearance of purity often takes precedence over honesty. A climate of pretence is thus created. In such societies, people feel the need to be perceived as good by others. When we feel the need to be seen to be good, like a frightened child, we will pretend in order to please.

Pretence kills more people than cancer.

We are not interested in such nonsense, however. Rather, we insist on honesty above purity, with no sense of self-judgement. You must make a pact with yourself not to judge as you observe. You must give to yourself unconditional acceptance – even if no one has ever given this to you.

No sensible person puts their head over the parapet

if they think they will be shot. Instead, they wisely stay hidden until it is safe to come out. Likewise, do not expect the awkward, angry and rejected parts of you to show themselves. If on their first tentative appearance you condemn them, hit out at them in shame and self-recrimination.

Our secrets and evasions need to be allowed to surface freely, for they are our teachers, much more than our supposed successes.

Take, for instance, the shop worker who gets angry when she does not get the break times she wants. It happens every day, but she does not notice it for a while. But when she does notice, she sees how much she is still trying to control the day, forcing the day into a shape made by her.

She has observed the familiar and simple – that her daily desire for control makes her unhappy. It is not particularly pleasant to see, but she has allowed it to the surface and let it be her teacher. She is on the path to happiness.

If we do not allow things to surface, they will stay buried, with all the anger and spite of the judged and rejected.

And in time they will have a terrible revenge.

\*

This is not a call to confess anything to anyone. That may be a possibility further down the line, if it is felt to be beneficial. Overall, however, the pressure of confession is counter-productive, for it creates a climate of fear or selectivity in issues faced. Much confession is a litany of things that don't need to be said, in order to avoid the things that do.

Until you wish them to be, the contents of your soul are no one else's business.

What is crucial is observation without judgement and without dread. The simplest and purest of flowers – the lotus of enlightenment – blossoms in the unlikeliest of places, the unhealthy mud of lowland swamps. The swamp becomes the lotus. The mire becomes beauty. Our unhappiness becomes our teacher. Existence is one.

*

Our sly ego will be concerned at this point and may well turn to ridicule. Perhaps, for instance, it will ridicule self-observation for being self-obsessed.

Nothing could be further from the truth, however. The self-obsessed would never dare observe themselves. Imagine what they might see! Self-observation is the opposite of self-worship. It is the most threatening of actions, inviting a painful dismantling of our cherished self-image.

Or perhaps the ego will play the moral crusader, and suggest that changing the world might be a little more useful than observing yourself.

But if you wish to change the world, then observing your self is the place to start.

You need do nothing else. If you want to stop the insanity in the world, pause and reflect on the only insanity you have any power over – your own. Observe yourself, and as your eyes gradually become accustomed to the dark, you will begin to see.

You might, for instance, see your manipulation of others. You are the cat rubbing at its owner's leg in calculated friendship.

You might begin to see your fear. This is the fear that either keeps you hidden from the action, or launches you into absurd aggression and hate.

You might also begin to see your judgement of others. This condemnation depersonalises people, demonising them, freeing you for all sorts of legitimate atrocity against them, whether mental, emotional or physical, whether private, local or international.

Manipulation, fear, control, and judgement – these are what you might see, as your eyes become accustomed to your hidden places. How could it be otherwise? These are the normal modes of animal and human relationship.

*

This explains why, after most revolutions, only one more thing is required: a further revolution. There is no system of government that can improve the lot of unexamined lives. Unexamined lives are asleep to all things. Such lives frequently know what they do *not* want, but do not know what they *do* want. So they may cry with passion and power, 'Reform the system!' But they can never *improve* the system. They can merely replace it with something that malfunctions in different ways.

For they themselves are the problem.

Supermarkets sometimes change the packaging of salads. It gives fresh visual impact. They don't change the salads themselves. The content is still the same. But the packaging is different. In the same way, we sometimes change governments.

Revolutions can execute the king. But they cannot execute transformation.

But we are not concerned here with political revolutions. Rather, we are concerned with the more significant revolution of self-observation. Once we have recognised and greeted manipulation, fear, control and judgement, we can begin to say goodbye to them. Once observed, the change can begin; once we are aware, half the battle is won.

*

The workplace is not always a happy place. Long-running hostilities often exist. People arrive at work knowing who they like and who they do not like. A splitting of humanity has quietly taken place, a separation of good and bad. We will display charity towards those whom we regard as good, but give little room to those deemed bad.

Self-observation quickly exposes such personal vendettas, however, and questions the low-grade happiness we experience in their pursuit. How different the day at work would be if we refused to split humanity, and started the day with a clean slate for all.

If the sea can twice daily wipe clean the beach, then once daily I can wipe clean the past.

\*

So don't try to change the world. Start instead to observe yourself. It will be a better use of your time. Those who are asleep can change many things but improve nothing.

The world is not the problem. As we shall discover later, the world is quite perfect. It is the reformers who are the problem, the activists who want to make external things better. They are not at home to themselves – but insist on trying to lead others home. This is why things stay the same. Solutions imposed from the outside are not solutions. They bring change – but not transformation. For you cannot promote transformation beyond the degree of internal transformation in yourself.

65

For such people, changing the world is less threatening than listening to themselves. Less threatening, and less necessary. In their hands, the more things change, the more things stay the same.

\*

A further reason why this instruction is to observe without judgement is that we are simply not fit to judge anything, neither ourselves nor anyone else.

I am sitting in a hotel. I have spent my first night there and come down now for breakfast. I notice a woman ordering her food. She wants tomatoes on toast, but without butter. She makes rather a fuss about it to the waitress. No butter! she says to the hapless girl. And I judge her. In my view, she's just another picky hotel guest, who doesn't know how lucky she is.

For my first two days there, I have the full English breakfast. But on the third day, aware of my expanding waist, I opt for their healthy option: tomatoes on toast. When it comes, however, it is anything but healthy. It is simply dripping with butter. I eat it, but remember.

When I am ordering the following day, I am keen to make the point to the waitress about the butter, which is the opposite of the healthy option. I probably make rather a fuss about it. No butter! I say to the hapless girl.

I sense the judgement of the newcomer to the hotel at the table next to me, as they order the full English.

Self-observation reveals us as people fit to judge nothing and no one. It is a liberating experience.

\*

People tend to judge from their sense of conscience. This is something generally encouraged. 'Listen to your conscience,' we are told. But this is not so simple, for we have not one conscience, but two, and they differ considerably. They are two twins, true conscience and learned conscience, but they speak with very different voices.

True conscience is a timeless place, a universal place, and one full of light, from which we can make clear, strong, present and just assessments. This true conscience is a clean and concise existence inside us as a possibility now, and many may already have experienced it.

We are more familiar, however, with its twin, learned conscience. Learned conscience is comprised of guidelines we have absorbed down the years. It is a place of half-light, an unchecked assortment of codes and messages, a bundle of unexamined assumptions, passed on to us by a variety of authority figures in our past, and which we now assume to be absolutely true.

This learned conscience is an eager judge on all matters, but not a reliable one. Its conclusions are random, but unquestioned by us. In listening to such conclusions, we are those setting out to travel the world in a second-hand car about which we know nothing. If we did know its history, we wouldn't dream of relying on it for our journey.

Sometimes people preface a judgement by saying 'in all conscience'. The question is: from which conscience do they speak, true or learned?

\*

Learned conscience is the jury from hell. In its power we become a group of disparate voices, gathered from our past. Each voice has its own agenda, shouting and posturing, but with no foreman to seek consensus or question overall direction. The unity of moral purpose we fondly imagine ourselves to embody is an illusion. As one psychiatrist wrote, 'One is evidently witness not to a single false self but to a number of only partially elaborated fragments of what might constitute a personality, if any single one had full sway. It seems best, therefore, to call the total of such elements a false-self system, or a system of false selves.'[2]

Our false selves comprise and compose our learned conscience.

But within us there exists a different place – a place of clarity and spontaneity, present only to accuracy and goodness. This is our true conscience, and it can

[2] R. D. Laing.

68

emerge if we dare curiosity concerning the origin of our selves.

*

Our learned conscience is considerably helped by our buffers, which work tirelessly to maintain our own sense of integrity and unity of being. It is their task to protect us from the contradictions within, which we are so loath to face. It was his psychological buffers that helped Stalin to return home for a pleasant tea with his daughter, after ordering the murder of ten other daughters that day. Buffers also allowed John to feel good about himself when he donated a pound to the African Children's Project – after spending a thousand pounds on sound equipment for himself. Thanks to his buffers, John thinks the world would be a better place if there were more generous people like him.

Stalin slept well at night, and so does John, courtesy of their buffers.

Buffers are a deft psychological trick, ensuring that we do not truly glimpse the nature of the chaos within. They enable us to believe what we want about ourselves. When, for instance, the head teacher acts vindictively against her deputy, out of jealousy, she calls it much-needed 'staff development', and feels wholly justified. Her buffers will leave her convinced.

And of course every driver is right.

We might for a moment feel unease behind the wheel after we have failed to indicate, causing anger in the car behind. Something like shame might break through briefly, with a moment of true seeing. But the moment passes. Our certainty is quickly re-established, doubts dispersed, and our illusion of personal integrity can live another day. 'They were driving much too close, anyway!'

\*

Buffers are not all bad. No one is all bad. Our buffers stop our mental train coming off the rails, causing carnage and chaos. If all our contradictions entered the room at the same time, if all our insanities, blindness and malice burst in upon us at once, we would not survive. We would disintegrate in the face of such savage exposure.

Buffers save us from this.

If our buffers were removed, we would see too much, we would weep at the sight of it, and look to the heavens for help. But with these blockers in place, there is no need for concern, for in our own minds we are the most reasonable people on earth. We are the clear voice of reason in an increasingly mad world.

Buffers are important for survival, but the enemy of growth, for they deny us true awareness.

\*

Sometimes in his lunch break, Tom would sit on a bench in the square, by the fountain. Here Tom would eat his sandwich and observe events and passers-by. He did not interfere. And he did not judge. He was content just to watch.

In such a manner, we are invited to observe ourselves.

Initially, we will primarily be observing our personality. Our true self is revealed more slowly. For this reason, initial observations may not be particularly flattering. Perhaps we will see less than beautiful things in ourselves as we allow the covers to be lifted on the simple and familiar.

But as with Tom on the bench by the fountain, we do not get involved. We just observe. We neither blame ourselves nor exonerate ourselves. We just watch.

*

Imagine a prison, and imagine a prisoner, incarcerated there for many years. And after all these years, the prisoner is delusional. He believes the prison building is all there is, that there is no world beyond. He wonders to himself if he was born in the prison. Certainly he can remember nothing else. The prison and he are one. Who is he? He is a prisoner. He imagines everyone's a prisoner as he cannot imagine a world outside a prison. This is how things are.

But now, with each stumbling step as he escapes –

why is he doing this?! – with each mile travelled in this bewildering new freedom, he is feeling something new. With each item of prison clothing discarded, the prisoner is gradually ceasing to be a prisoner.

What he was becoming he didn't know, but at least he now knew what he was not. He was not a prisoner. As he glanced back, the prison seemed such a small place. How could he have allowed that to be his world for so long? He decided to put as much distance as he could between that place and himself.

Better the devil you know?

Not at all.

*

Our remorseless identification with the prison of our personality leads us into lives of tedious repetition, as dull as a thrice-told tale. Our lives may appear to change, but our interactions don't. Hence the famous monk who left one monastery after another because he just did not get on with the people there. In the end he had to admit that the only common denominator in his repeated unhappiness was himself. Yet all the time, as he looked back on his life, he had really imagined himself free; and if you had asked him then, if he was a prisoner to himself, he would have found you faintly ridiculous.

We live in what is sometimes called the 'Free World'.

It is perhaps surprising, therefore, that there are so few truly free people.

*

I listen to someone tell me that they are down today because it has been cloudy, they have had a bad day at work, and have had no cards from friends recently. This is what they tell me and it is a sad human tale.

Yet their sadness is entirely of their own making. They are like those who choose to walk on thin ice, and then despair when they fall in. It is not that the sun, professional fulfilment or friends cannot give pleasure. They can give great pleasure. It is simply that they do not make us who we are. So why should we be sad?

We receive the mental message that it is cloudy, and turn it into depression. We receive the mental message of a bad day at work and turn it into self-pity. We receive the mental message of disappointing friends, and turn it into resentment.

We get a thousand mental messages every day. Our mistake is to turn them into emotions.

Such things are not a basis for a mood. A life lived in the thrall of one meaningless mood after another is a treadmill of automatic reaction, and a sign of how far we are from home.

*

Your day had been going well. You were upbeat and charming to everyone. And then everything was ruined when you received what you felt to be a slight from your colleague. Intentional or not, it was hurtful and soon it was crystallising into something heavy inside, and gnawing.

This is why we need the inner observer. The inner observer sees the mood, and asks questions. The observer understands the origins of this crystallising heaviness, but looks also at the destructive cost to the self. This is chosen unhappiness.

The inner observer asks questions only that one day we might travel more freely through the world.

*

And so the second commandment is to observe yourself, to divide your attention between doing what you must do and watching yourself doing it. But we do this gently – as one sitting by a fountain in their lunch break, watching the world go by.

*Today, I will declare an amnesty on all my assumptions, everything I think I know about what I should and shouldn't do, and what others should and shouldn't do. It will be a day of complete and utter freedom, and even as I join the queue with my bag of all sorts, my fear at what I might discover is tempered by the cheerful and relieved laughter I hear from those ahead of me.*

# 3

# Be Nothing

*'From the beginning, not a thing is.'*

Hui Neng

The normal observation when gazing up at the big night sky is something like this: 'Aren't the stars fantastic tonight?' But, as with most normal observations, we are missing the point. And the point is the space. The stars would be nothing without that wonderful dark space in which they live, move and have their being.

Something only shines in the context of nothing.

\*

We like the presence of things. We like the presence of colour, the presence of taste, the presence of ideas, or the presence of friends. Sex is presence. Art is presence. Sport is presence. Presence fills our world in bright, stimulating, solid, exciting, reassuring ways. It is hard to imagine anything more important than presence.

But absence is more important than presence, for absence is the cradle in which presence is laid.

\*

A woman wandered around the home she was soon to leave. She was moving house, and all things had now been removed. Her car waited outside. She could leave at any time. Her furniture had gone, every scrap of it. The curtains, carpets, bed, sofa, radio, music centre, pictures, telly, photos, books, cooker, chairs, bath mat, DVDs, toothbrush, bedside table, knick-knacks, cushions, lucky monkey. Everything. With all now stripped bare, there was only the clunky echo as she walked across the bare floorboards.

As she looked around, it was almost as if she'd never been here at all. All that she had built, created, used, lived through, was gone. Her mind was a cinema of everything that had happened in this place – the events, experiences, people and emotions. The crises, the happiness, the struggle, loneliness and laughter. It was like standing on a stage after the show, when everyone had gone. So much lived! She could hear the moments as well as see them, smell them as well as feel them. For years, her front door had opened on to a little world she had created. She would return every day, turn the key, push open the door, and there it was, so full of her and who she was and what she valued.

But no more. For now that world was packed up, boxed up, and gone. And she was left with just this shell.

So why didn't she just drive away? Why prolong this sad, lingering death? Why not just be done with it, close her eyes, close her heart, walk out, shut the door behind her and leave? She couldn't. She had to stay. She had to face the emptiness and acknowledge the void. She had to allow herself to live the space left by the absence of all her things, to live the space now free from the clutter, the sparse space that had quietly held it all, the space she had never really noticed until now.

The presence of things she *had* noticed, the absence of things she had not. She had feared space, if she was honest. That's why every nook and cranny had been filled. But now, strange to report, each room was for her a hallowed and gracious absence in which presence had merely come to stay for a while. Presence never stayed for ever. But absence was always there. 'From the beginning, not a thing is.' Yes.

She hugged in her heart the beautiful nothing, which had created so much, and hosted so much. She breathed it, wondered at it, moved in awe of it, walking gently from room to room, seeing and feeling each one afresh. The absence was her friend. She had dreaded it for months, but discovered there was nothing to fear. The absence had been her friend all these years, quietly holding all. If this was death, then let her die some more. No more would she fear the empty email screen or the silent phone.

It was time now for her to go. She picked up her bag, took the car keys for the final time from the cleared mantelpiece, and then opened the door on to her new world. She had a life to live.

Non-existence is prior to existence, and void is prior to fullness. The woman thought her home had gone, but discovered that was far from the case, for the essence of her home was the space. Before presence, absence. Before her furniture, the emptiness. Only the emptiness remained. In time, it would create again.

*

There is no anticipation quite so keen as that created by emptiness, and no possibility so pure as that of the clean slate. The empty plate awaits food, the empty beer glass awaits filling. In their emptiness, they are miracles waiting to happen.

It is strange, therefore, that we fear emptiness.

The starting point for every marvel is absence, and the launch pad of possibility is always nothing, out of which something may occur. Nothing is the foundation for life, because nothing is pre-existent, while something is not. Something is the new kid in town. Charming – but passing through.

When we lose sight of these things, we tend to panic. Emptiness becomes the enemy, and nothing becomes something to fear. Think of the woman who needed an event in her diary every night, or she panicked. Think of the man who liked his wall covered in stimulating posters, fearing any gaps.

When we assume fullness to be normal, we become afraid and anxious when we do not experience it. Something comes to be seen as more important than nothing, because something is colourful and distracting.

Absence isn't news. But it is only absence that creates the event. The songwriter who wishes it could be Christmas every day does not understand this. Christmas is Christmas because for most of the time it isn't.

Without absence, there is no presence, without the darkness, no twinkling stars.

*

We fill our day with activity. We turn on the radio as we make the toast. We feel awkward in silence.

The idea of nothing happening is so terrifying that people will go to almost any lengths to ensure it is not so. They will turn on the telly, have a baby or take on extra work – anything to keep the phone ringing, the moments filled and silence at bay.

Any thing is better than no thing, it seems.

*

It is the work of the ego to create fear of absence. Absence gives nothing for the ego to manipulate. The ego can work with anything. But it cannot work with nothing.

The opposite is true for our essence, however, our true self. For our true self, absence is the dawn of adventure.

Sometimes we have very bad days, when everything we hoped for fails to happen. Or things that we dread do happen. We feel demolished, tearful and without hope. There is nothing good here. We just feel empty.

Genius takes many forms. The genius here is to allow the emptiness. This is the skilful attitude. The emptiness is the porchway to our true self, which is untouched by the day. Our personality is understandably distraught, but our true self has a life so complete that it is untouched by the disappointments that trouble our path. The emptiness will take us there if we allow it.

Before presence, absence. Before ego, no-ego.

*

Imagine stepping off a treadmill. You have been running on a treadmill for so long, but you have decided to step off. And now you are walking across the grass towards the edge of the cliff, to leap into a gorgeous void. After so much meaningless and exhausting activity – for meaningless activity is particularly exhausting – you long to throw yourself into the strange holding of nothing. Will you dare?

The ego is running after you, telling you not to be so stupid, that you'd be mad to jump, to stay on the treadmill at all costs. He says you will kill yourself if you jump. He says there's nothing there. He asks how can you wish for nothing when the treadmill works so well?

What do you say? What do you do?

*

'Don't think, but look,' said an eminent philosopher.[3] Thinking can be clever, but only seeing is true. Truth exists beyond tired mental constructions, beyond thought.

It is possible, particularly in the West, that we have been a little slow to question our minds, if indeed we have questioned them at all. We have perhaps imagined them as all-reasonable, all-sensible guides for our journey through life. To question the way we think would be to

[3] Ludwig Wittgenstein.

question the unquestionable, and think the unthinkable. Does the flamingo question its one working leg? Not unless it wants to fall over and look stupid. And likewise, we do not question our minds. 'The human mind is a marvel!' we all declare. 'If anything can take us to new places, then surely the mind will!'

But it is not so. It is our minds that separate us from our truest selves.

Our minds are indeed remarkable tools. The technical intelligence of the human mind is staggering, and in itself a gift. But the mind needs to know its place. It is the tool – not the craftsman. A tool is a tool – something to be used by another, but not something that should be allowed to use itself. When the tool thinks it's the craftsman, there is a problem.

And that is the state of our mind at present. We are not using it. It is using us.

Far from being a path to fresh life, our thinking is a cul-de-sac, which merely turns us round and about, returning us back to where we came from. It has no access to the territory beyond our personality, and how could it? Why should we have ever hoped it might? The mind cannot take us where it hasn't been itself, because our thought is history. Our thought is merely a response of our past. It is borrowed from the unexamined influence of others, experiences long forgotten, and programmed slowly but surely by events repeated over and over again. Our thoughts are pickled in history, and forever old. How could such an entrapped creature point us to freedom?

*

Talk like this is sometimes called the Negative Way – the path of silence and void. It is the path more concerned with things that are not than with things that apparently are. It is the path that does not fear nothing, for it knows that all good comes from there. And it is the path that, unlike thought, *does* lead us to the territory beyond, a path that crosses impossible canyons of inner estrangement.

Perhaps our biggest fear, as we face such a path, is that we will cease to exist. If I welcome absence, if I am content to be empty, and less in the grip of thought – then who will I be?

There is no need to panic. Nothing good was ever lost in the pursuit of truth. How could anyone as essentially authentic as you be diminished by engaging with reality? You will not cease to be, for you cannot cease to be. Your inner essence is indestructible and eternal. A lot of mental nonsense, which you have mistakenly identified with, might cease to be, but then this mental nonsense has nothing to do with you anyway. It does not define who you are – it actually separates you from who you are.

How can you cease to be when your best self, your essence, is for the first time being found?

As we let go of the old, the future will quietly fill the

inner space created. It is in this space between our thoughts that we begin to grow. It is in the space between thoughts that we discover what it is to be awake, to be conscious. And far from seeing less clearly, we find that by-passing our borrowed mental constructs actually creates space. As a fourteenth-century mystic said, 'To one who knows nothing, it is clearly revealed,'[4] and so it is.

Against a pure white screen within, silhouettes are discerned clear and sharp as they come and go. It is seeing. But not thinking. The paralysing complexities so beloved of our busy minds simplify themselves not into answers but awareness. The mad pendulum of extremes begins to settle in the centre place, where all things can be held. We are now seeing through things and into things as opposed to looking *at* things. It is not old history-bound thinking, but fresh attention, the possibility of new experience, clearly perceived and free from our weary and stale agendas.

This is what it is to *be*. This is what it is to *be silent*, liberated from our chattering thoughts. This is what it is to be empty – open to possibility of true adventure. This is what it is to be void – a deep inner hollow of indescribable light and beauty. To be or not to be? That is the daily question.

\*

[4] Meister Eckart.

We may need to remove some armour fully to enjoy the experience – the armour of incessant mental and emotional activity. We feel such things essential to keep at bay feelings of emptiness. We imagine that, if we remove this armour, something terrible will happen to us. But not all armour is good, as David famously discovered when he took on the giant Goliath. Being younger and considerably smaller than his opponent, David had been loaded with armour by others. He was told that he would need it, that it was absolutely essential in circumstances like this. They were older than him. They knew. Only a young fool would take one step outside the tent without it.

But in himself David knew that the armour would have to come off. He couldn't move in it. It made sense to the world, but not to him. And so it was that he faced Goliath not with the baggage of others weighing him down – he had left that in the tent – but simply with what he himself knew.

It wasn't a contest. Or rather it was – but it was a short one.

*

I once worked in a community centre when the Queen came to visit. A day full of presence, full of colour, crowds, and excitement. Cameras flashed, TV reporters roamed, and people cheered.

But when I look back on the day, I do not really remember any of that, fine though it was. What I do remember is sitting alone in the space early in the morning, pondering the emptiness that was about to create so much, the space so full of potential. It took me some years to realise that what was true of a building awaiting the Queen was true also of myself.

And so I am learning to start with absence, and learning that nothing rules. For much can be made of nothing. But nothing can be made of much.

*Today, I will be space. My interior will be a large hallway of emptiness, into which people can come if they wish. They can pass through, but they cannot stay. I have nothing to offer them but the space, and nothing to draw on but the space. It is suddenly as if I don't know anything, and yet don't need to know anything.*

*The vast emptiness has its own authority.*

# 4

## Flee Attachment

*'Most people are enclosed in their mortal bodies like snails in their shells, curled up in their obsessions after the manner of hedgehogs.'*

Clement of Alexandria

The parent sits down to watch the school play. Their child is performing, and they have made the costume themselves. They sit in the audience and watch. They are restless for the appearance of their child. They are some way into the performance and still no sign. They begin to get irritated by the other performers hogging the stage. They want their own child to shine.

They are restless now, not noticing very much at all. Certainly they do not notice the child in tears, who missed his cue and came on late. They have eyes only for their child, in the costume they made!

The virtuous parent identifies with their child. What could be more natural? But such attachment is unwise. Attachment makes us blind. Identifying colours our perceptions. We become blind people who notice nothing and enjoy nothing. We become the plaything of our ego.

\*

I have benefited from many spiritual teachers, with different-coloured skins, different native tongues, and different meals on their tables at night. Yet they all told me the same thing, and what they told me was this: 'Stop doing what you are doing. And good will grow.'

'Is that it? I ask inwardly, imagining that these must merely be opening lines, with much more still to come. 'No, that's it,' they say. 'Stop doing what you are doing, and good will grow.'

But what am I doing?

Surprisingly, this is not a question often asked. It is asked on a superficial level. Someone I haven't seen for a while might ask what I am doing these days. Or a policeman might ask me what I am doing with the matches and the petrol at midnight in my ex-boss's shed on the allotment. These things are asked.

But the spiritual teachers are looking at a profounder form of doing. For what are we doing the most? We are attaching ourselves to things. We do this relentlessly. And attachment makes us blind.

We are identifying with our mother. We are identifying with our religion. We are identifying with our partner. We are identifying with our atheism. We are identifying with our self-image. We are identifying with our children. We are identifying with our gender, with our work, our culture, our moods, our country, our past, our feelings, our football team. We choose the focus of our passion, identify accordingly, and consign everyone else to hell.

Take the boss in the office who tells everyone at the beginning of the day that they should tread carefully around him, because he is in a very bad mood. The boss is attached to his mood, as if it was something real.

Meanwhile, the terrorist can't hear the screams, because he's identifying with his cause, while the nurse is being awkward with everybody, because she has no partner at present, and imagines that she must therefore be unhappy.

When we attach, we cease to be open and generous towards creation, opting instead for a sensible bigotry. Attachment leaves us fighting a corner – rather than loving the world.

My football team is everything! I love them! Every other team is rubbish! I hate them!

I am stupid. I am normal. I fit in well with the way things are.

*

We will also be cautious about attaching ourselves to the word 'love', for the word has lost its way. Its origins are fine. Openness towards all is the spring from which love once flowed. But it has become polluted by the ego, and cut off from its source. From being an attitude to life that acknowledges all as equal, and lives the ultimate oneness of reality, blessing all and favouring no one, it has become a high-voltage emotion, something possessive and jealous and therefore never far from hate.

Openness has become a controlling and localised emotion called 'love'. Love is now shorthand for something untouched by wonder.

*

Take the mother who loved her child so much that she wanted him to be top of his class at everything. Day after day, she made it very plain. 'You must come first. It's for your own good, your own self-respect and future.' Unfortunately, every other mother with children in that class loved their children in the same way. And day after day, they also made it plain to their children. 'You must come first. It's for your own good, your own self-respect and future.'

Unfortunately, not everyone can come first, and so it is hard for children caught up in such 'love'. They will grow up unable to cope with failure, for love in their experience has always been linked to success.

The invitation here is to cherish all things – but flee attachment, because we hurt people by it. All manner of evil is possible in those who identify in such a way. It is narrowing of scope and possibility.

*

There are so many things with which we should not identify that it is hard to know where to start.

We are constantly tempted to identify with knowledge, but knowledge in itself has no significance, unless it is transforming. There has never been a more informed generation on this planet – or a less transformed one. The mysterious energies that turn hate, greed and delusion into compassion, generosity and awareness do not lie in knowing more things. Rather, in understanding more things.

We will also be wary of identifying with the word 'God', and attaching ourselves to this God's cause. Belief in a deity who gives the seal of sacred approval to our own selves can sometimes root within us a dangerous and self-damaging damaging egotism, an egotism that can't help but get up in the morning and think it is right.

All truly destructive people wake in the morning feeling they are right.

If you are sure you are right, you are wrong.

The enlightened go to religion not to gain something but to lose something. They do not go to religion for accreditation but dismantling. They go there to be led into the confusion, which leads to true clarity. Stop doing what you are doing – and good will grow. This is why most spiritual growth is about dismantlement, not acquisition. With psychic impediments taken away, the discovery is this: the human soul will naturally lead us home to our truest selves.

\*

We have already been warned away from identifying with our past, because although it was formative it no longer has power, unless we grant it that power. The past made us, but it does not define us. As one teacher said, 'I want to ask you: can you look at yourself today without the eyes of the past? Where there is no past, there is bliss in the present moment.'[5]

We will not identify with our emotions, which leave us demented with stupidity, and unable to see things as they are. Against the white of non-identification, all things are clearly perceived. But the strong colours of emotion smear the white. The present is white and the keeper of all things. The white holds the colours, like a snake expert holds a viper.

When we identify with emotions, the colours become keepers of themselves, all spillage and mess, like watercolours in the rain.

[5] Krishnamurti.

\*

In particular, we will not identify with our negative emotions. This will be hard, because we are very fond of them. They are our first love. We enjoy disliking people, and experience huge pleasure in finding someone else who dislikes them in the same way. We buy newspapers that share our dislikes.

Yet it is not your true self that dislikes. It is your unexamined past. The negative turbulence in you does not come from any authentic place within. So you do not need to identify with these emotions. You have the right not to be negative.

We identify with negative emotions more than anything else. The list of negative emotions is not a short one. Suspicion, vanity, resentment, self-pity, anxiety, self-justification, fear, anger, judgement all catch us in their compelling web. Yet not one of these emotions was there when we were born. Which begs a significant question: where have they come from?

Over time, we have acquired them without knowing. We have absorbed attitudes around us. These negative emotions are illusory layers of understanding imposed on us by others, and have nothing to do with who we are. The negative emotion is not you. You have a right not to be negative. You have a right to reclaim your birthright.

*

There is a dark intelligence in negativity.

Those in a negative state know best how to hurt others. Instinctively, they know where people are vulnerable. They will hurt you with their attacks.

There are many forms of genius and the genius here is not to identify with their attacks.

The negativity of others can hit us with almost physical force. But instead of taking the hit painfully in the chest, become a swirling vapour through which all passes. Refuse to identify with it, let it pass through you, leaving no trace of resentment within. The people who do such things – they are asleep. They don't know what they do. Just as I do not know what I do, and you do not know what you do. So refuse to identify either with your negativity or theirs.

It has been wisely said that as long as we are joined with someone in a negative state we cannot know them. We cannot know anyone in a state of anger, bitterness, jealousy or resentment.

*

It is sometimes imagined that, if we do not identify with people or things or issues in the traditional manner, we will not play a full part in the world. It is imagined that we will be as cold fish, swimming distantly around the edge of painful life, remote, passionless and ultimately useless.

But such things are imagined only by the ego, and the ego is a liar. Such thoughts as these have a certain sneering energy, but they are not true. We understand the ego's desperation. But we don't have to applaud it.

The truth, as always, lies elsewhere. Freeing ourselves from identification, we engage more fully with the world, not because of what we do, but because of what we are. As we begin to shed our conditioning, a new reality grows within us, which will gradually spill over into surrounding circumstances.

It is a pleasure to see the child in the park free of attachment. She watches the sparkly fountain, captivated and in awe. It has her fullest attention, until the pigeon arrives. She then turns towards this feathered wonder, and follows it in a little dance around the water, chasing and happy. When the pigeon flies away, she is left alone, and looks across to the wall where her father sits. Reassured by his presence, she spots an acorn on the ground, and sits down, in order to investigate this most surprising thing.

Once free of attachment, we look on the world with a child's eyes, in which everything is new, and nothing is the same. We experience a direct knowledge of things as they are, free from manipulative, clinging and stale agendas. We embody openness, refusing favourites. We are open to all, and to bless all. Passionate, involved, dying even, but identifying with nothing. Not even with death.

Cherish all things – but attach to none.

*

And now it is important to contradict ourselves because, when we have boxed truth, it must break out and declare us stupid. So we say something is absolutely true, until it isn't.

So do not become attached. Attach yourself to your essence.

*

We face a problem as we contemplate our essence. Higher states of existence are not best described by words. An interviewer once asked the dancer Pavlova what her dance meant. 'If I could speak it, I wouldn't have danced it,' she replied. People paint pictures, compose music and sculpt stone because words are inadequate for the expression of profounder truths.

What chance of words describing our essence, therefore?

We have one ace in our pack, however – our experience. We know this creature already. We sense inside ourselves already this prowling lion of powerful possibility. Our essence is not an abstract and elusive idea

96

like some portrayals of heaven. Rather, it is something we already know. We have all experienced our essence, and are acquainted with some of its attributes. We may wish to know it better, but we are certainly acquainted. As we contemplate our essence, we will be struck by significant recognition.

For our essence is the reality in the centre of our being. It is our truest self. It has been described by one writer as a reservoir of sweetness, warmth, kindness, empathy, clarity, discernment, intelligence, synthesis, will, steadfastness, commitment, contact, gentleness, subtlety, refinement, openness, curiosity, happiness, enjoyment, balance, courage, justice, detachment, precision, objectivity, spaciousness, expansion, depth, capacity, initiative, passion, fulfilment, contentment, generosity, and identity.[6]

These are startling qualities, and the primary energies within us.

But like graffiti scrawled across a masterpiece, secondary energies, created by our personalities, often overwhelm us. Energies like despair, pride, judgement, negativity, resentment, anger, fear, vanity, jealousy, depression and anxiety have their own bleak force within us. We learnt these things well when young, and unlearning childhood lessons is hard.

But these energies remain secondary to who we are. Primary to who we are is our essence.

[6] A. H. Almaas.

97

\*

It is a good day when we attach ourselves to our essence. It is a good day when it is our essence, our essential nature, that makes an impression on us, when it is this to which we are loyal. It is the most fruitful of meetings, when our ego meets our essence, just as in our past it has been the most harmful of partings.

Our ego, in its own frightened manner, is trying to find the way home. But it is very lost.

\*

And so it is that we become uncurled from our obsessions to which we are attached. We identify less with emotion, and find ourselves more conscious of people. We identify less with our body, and find ourselves more conscious of spirit.

*Today I will remember that my true colour is no colour – the no-colour that makes all other colours brilliant. Being no colour, I can receive all colours, and be all colours. No particular colour will claim me for its own. But neither will any colour be turned away.*

# 5

## Transcend Suffering

*'Our happiness is deep-rooted and real;*
*while our despair is shallow-rooted and*
*unreal, born of delusion and ignorance.*
*We suffer because we overlook the fact*
*that we are all right.'*

D. E. Harding

As the great piano player leaves the stage after the performance, the well-wisher rushes towards him, and declares from the bottom of his heart, 'You're so lucky to be able to play the piano like that!' 'Yes,' replies the great piano player, 'eight-hours'-practice-a-day lucky.'

And here I am, in another place and another time, rushing up to the Enlightened One, for I have always wished to meet someone truly enlightened. And I am wondering at her serenity, at the nature of her Being, and declaring from the bottom of my heart, 'How wonderful to be so enlightened, so awake, so conscious!'

'Yes,' replies the Enlightened One, 'the-transformation-of-suffering wonderful.'

\*

When suffering comes, we have a choice that is both simple and significant: to resent or to accept it? Whether it is justified suffering or not is irrelevant. You might be a murderer spending your first night in jail, or you might be a social worker hit by a drunk driver. On the face of it, the first was to blame for their predicament, the second was not, but the choice remains the same: to resent or accept?

If we resent pain, as everything in us screams that we should, we follow the well-worn path of negativity. If we accept pain, the miracle of transformation begins: the transformation of suffering.

The East and West have taken rather different paths in these matters. And these paths have led to different discoveries.

The remarkable technological advances in the West in the last 600 years have been the fruit of the pursuit of knowledge in an intellectual climate where suffering is regarded as an interruption to life.

The remarkable psychological advances in the East over the last 2,500 years have been the result of a philosophy that seeks to transcend suffering, in a climate that regards suffering as something that just *is*, and seeks to go forward from that realisation.

The rationalist tradition in the West imagines that, with one more technological breakthrough, we can alter reality. The East says that a warthog will tell you the time in seven languages before reality changes.

The West says we can change things from the outside – just look at the strides forward in medicine! The East insists that we can change things only on the inside, through different attitudes within.

\*

In a locked room, a man is chained to the wall.

He is a hostage. Caught up in a game played by others, he is powerless and innocent. It is said he will die, unless his government negotiates, but there is little hope of that. The other hostages have been killed. And he will be next. When he thinks back to times past, he is over-come with self-pity. When he thinks ahead, inventing outcomes both pleasing and dire, he is tortured by his meaningless hallucinating.

Then the door is opened and a hand is held out to him. He is offered an orange by a friendly young jailer. He regards it as an insult, and pushes it away in anger. The jailer presses it into his hand, and again the captive waves it away. As if *he* was ever going to accept a gift from that hateful person! As if this prison guard could honestly expect him to accept his situation, to acquiesce in his confinement, and eat that fruit, as if nothing was wrong, as if everything was fine.

To accept it would be to give in, surrender his will. He would never accept it! So the jailer places the orange by the man's side, and leaves the room. The man weeps. He has nowhere to go, neither in the past, nor the future, nor the present.

After a while, he reaches out for the orange. He peels it and allows himself to eat it. It tastes good. He permits himself to enjoy the taste, to receive the light and goodness in his situation. He had been overlooking the fact that he was all right.

*

Legend has it that Earth is the Ridiculous or Lunatic planet. Many poets, artists and philosophers have echoed such thoughts, and we are familiar with their ideas. What is life but a tale told by an idiot, signifying nothing? And who are the gods, but those who torture for their own entertainment? We live a life, but without the feeling of being alive. We live the scream of despair, trapped in the terrors of being human. We are the insubstantial ones, the done-to ones, the hopeless ones. We are the hollow men, who live the short fall from the womb to the tomb, and are then no more. All is vanity, and earth the lunatic asylum of the universe.

We know such harsh forces in ourselves. These writers

speak on our behalf, and maybe the best of us scream at the darkening sky, the deep night and the beating rain. Maybe before we can accept anything we must scream until we can scream no more.

*

The difference between the rejection of suffering and the acceptance of suffering is trust. If, somewhere within us, there is a sense of trust, a sense of ultimate goodness, a sense of holding, then we can experience the pain as a messenger of some sort, an angel even, who wishes us no harm, but rather wills our good. If, however, we are not able to find such trust within us, then that same event will be experienced very differently.

There is a deep chasm between trust and no trust. To live on one side is a bleak and angry struggle. To live on the other, the beginnings of acceptance and the growing awareness that all things can be good.

*

Imagine the fearless hopeful soul for whom it is possible to be happy with all circumstances. A fearless hopeful soul which finds things perfect as they are. There would be in them no wistful thoughts about how good things used to be. Neither would there be any vague imaginings concerning how good things might be in the future. There would simply be the present with all its potential.

Is that possible? Is it possible that your soul could live the dark and light as equals, as one and the same thing? If that were possible, it would be the finest of all things, and there are voices across the continents and down the centuries that claim that such possibility is yours.

This is territory beyond the remarkable advances in the world of medicine. This is territory beyond the cure and the gracious alleviation of pain of modern technology. This is territory where each must travel alone, beyond the reach of both friends and science, into the heart of what it is to be human, what it is to face unasked for and unjust suffering – and to transform it into something good.

*

It has been said that life breaks us all but that some are made strong at the broken places. This is true, and a mystery. What is it that makes some strong and others not?

Certainly, there is nothing transforming in suffering itself. Neither is there any essential beauty in pain. Far from it. Pain and suffering are the scream of dislocated creation. We do not celebrate suffering, nor do we invite it.

The chemistry of possibility, however, lies in our reaction to it. It is here we can become alchemists turning dross into gold. For just as our unexamined suffering was the cause of much that is phoney in us, so accepted suffering, suffering transcended, is part of our journey home to that which is truthful within us.

But it all starts at the fork in the road, with resentment leading one way, and acceptance the other. We will travel both, but which shall we love the more?

Certainly they do not lead to the same place.

\*

I do not elevate one form of suffering above another, and I do not believe in a scale of suffering in which only the very highest scores should be taken seriously. Suffering is suffering and we should not evade our own, merely because someone is worse off than ourselves.

Let us listen to a man. He is a depressed man, probably imagining himself virtuous as he tells us that really he has nothing to complain about, given that many people in the world are homeless. How wonderful that someone can think in this way!

But this is not wonderful. Here is someone evading responsibility. If he has nothing to complain about, why is he so depressed? What anger has he buried and why? It is unlikely that he is doing much to solve the homelessness problem. It is more likely that he is merely avoiding the implications of facing the suffering on his own doorstep. The only suffering we can truly alleviate is our own.

To hide behind the suffering of others is evasion.

\*

The only suffering I can do anything with is my own. Each day I must choose either rejection or acceptance. If, for instance, I do not consciously accept that someone's attitude has hurt me, if I brush it off with a shrug of my shoulders and a 'Who cares?' – then my revenge when it comes will be unconscious and all the worse for that.

Or hear the former sports enthusiast now paralysed from the waist down after a climbing accident. How does he feel? He has no feelings about the matter, he tells me. He is a believer in God: 'If the Good Father willed it, then who am I to complain? Father knows best.'

He was the most angry of men. It never reached the surface, but seeped like acid inside him, killing relationship and happiness.

Rejection of suffering, and denial of its effects on us, turns the darkness in on ourselves, and locks us into internal patterns of destruction. Acceptance of it brings light into the darkness of our misery.

Misery fades because it has no true existence.

Tears dry because they possess no eternity.

\*

Buddha, Socrates and Jesus, in their different ways, all chose acceptance of suffering, and all, by their actions, transcended suffering's random and unjust assault on their lives.

Who they were and what they stood for grew out of their suffering – out of the transformation of their suffering, which is where we began this chapter. The crown of thorns, pressed viciously down, screams both the royalty and agony of suffering.

The hard question is not the oft asked, 'How can there be a God with all this suffering?' but rather, 'How can there be a human without it?' There is no clear route from childhood to consciousness that does not take in the dismantling darkness, the life-changing visitation of suffering. We will never get used to these visits. We will always feel the terror anew. We will certainly never seek suffering.

But we may also hear the words, 'Fear Not' when suffering comes. These things are possible.

*

I am standing on frozen ground, amidst the grip of icy cold. It is winter, and the wind moans, and the chill penetrates my hurting fingers. The soil is hard and bare beneath my feet.

Yet it is here, in these bleak days of snow and frost, that the earth finds rest. The rest is profound and transformative, and one from which it emerges most full of energy for growth.

At the heart of our experience of life is a cold winter. We need not fear the winter. It is always a fork in the road.

*Today I accept that I am one of the suffering, for where else did my negativity come from? This being so, I will be gentle with myself as I decide how to react in the face of pain or upset. The world waits to see which way I will jump, which attitude I will reach for.*

*By lunchtime, the world should have some answers.*

# 6

## Drop Your Illusions

*Someone put you on a slave block,*
*And the unreal brought you.*
*Now I keep coming to your owner saying,*
*'This one is mine.'*
*Don't worry, I will not let sadness possess*
  *you.*
*I will gladly borrow all the gold I need*
*To get you back.*

Hafiz

We do not like being told what to do, and we might
have good reason for this. Who knows what nonsense
people have told you in your past? You had to obey
then, for you were too vulnerable to do anything else.
But now? Now things have changed, and you watch very
closely when people tell you what to do.

So when someone says, 'Drop your illusions,' our first thought is almost certainly negative. Just who is this person to say that? They don't even know me! We then start mentally listing our achievements, and wondering how we could have done all that if we were deluded. We know some people are deluded – the mad, bad and sad. But not us. From where we are standing, there is simply nothing to drop.

*

It is hard to accept that there is nothing to acquire, but much to let go of. It is hard because our mind desires acquisition. We like acquisition. It creates a reassuring sense of progress and stimulation. And if my mind isn't acquiring, then what exactly is its purpose?

Yet the acquisition of knowledge never changes anyone.

Whilst the letting go of attitudes does.

The acquisition of knowledge threatens nothing untrue.

The letting go of attitudes threatens everything untrue.

Most of us is untrue.

No wonder we prefer acquisition.

*

A religious leader was talking about the temptations and dangers of giving people what they want to hear. He illustrated this thought by referring to the democracies of the world: 'Democracies run the risk that those eager for power will flatter the people. An adolescent who is endlessly flattered grows up to be a very disagreeable person, living a perception of themselves as the repository of all goodness and something that cannot be improved. A cult of self-flattery allied to a sentimental understanding of common humanity – well, such things when they concern the most powerful nations in the world are dire.'

Democracies boast a large number of insecure and vain people and so do we as individuals. We have a large number of insecure and vain people within us, and each of them is a dedicated lover of the flattery.

It is hard to vote for the end of such flattery. It is like voting for the end of medicine or crumpets. And we will find it hard initially to thank those who attempt to break our ties with our dream world, and tell us to drop our illusions, just as we might resent the window cleaner whose early moves with the cloth and bucket leave the rest of our glass looking a complete disgrace in comparison. What is he doing? It looks terrible!

But like all who expose illusions, the window cleaner is only giving back to us our true light and our true view. When he is finished, we feel the difference. The windows were dirty but now they are clean, and it's better. You hadn't realised what a negative aura the dirty glass gave to the whole room, and the view beyond. They were like a second set of blinds.

But now? Now, the view is amazing.

*

First, we are going to drop the illusion that we can do, and in our doing, control. We are going to attempt to get rid of the illusion that you and I are determining the nature of things around us, that we are creating and organising, making things better. We are going to drop the illusion that we are living our life, deciding its direction, controlling affairs.

Because we are not doing things – things are being done to us. And instead of us living life, life is living us.

Much of our experience is beyond our control. We do not choose to be born, for instance. Neither do we choose the country in which we are born, nor the social status. We do not choose the era of history in which we are born. We do not choose our parents. We do not choose our mental, emotional or physical intelligence. We do not choose our early life and formative influences. We do not choose our bodies. We do not choose to be well or to be ill. We do not choose our children. We do not choose the random. We do not choose to grow old. We do not choose to lose our faculties, and we do not choose to die.

These are things over which we have no control. These things are done to us.

Some will have a reply. Some will say that we do not choose the cards in our hands. But we can choose how to play them.

In my experience, however, good cards do the winning, and bad cards do the losing, and the only freedom we have is to understand the cards we hold. We do not love. We do not hate. We do not desire and we do not decide. Events carry us along as the wave carries the surfer. If we do not understand this, there is only rigidity as we try to force things, prove things, correct things, decide and define things, as our ego wishes and needs.

But if we *do* understand this, if we do accept that life is flowing beneath us and through us, uninvited and uncontrollable, then we can make room for it, create space for it, and allow for the beautiful unfolding.

Once understood, this is a great relief, both for ourselves and for those with whom we deal. We will neither attempt to chisel circumstances into a particular shape, nor chisel people into a particular shape.

We are not in control. Neither should we desire to be.

*

Second, we are going to drop the illusion that we are conscious and have free will.

We are not conscious. In the West, this observation goes against the grain. For Western psychology has tended to treat people as though they were conscious, and able to work through their problems. Eastern psychology, however, has regarded people as asleep, but dreaming they are conscious and with free will.

The evidence from self-observation is that the conclusions of the East are more compelling. How could we be considered conscious when so much of our lives is spent revisiting the non-existent past, or pondering the non-existent future? These are the obsessions of the unconscious. It is a similar story with the act of judgement. You cannot judge another and at the same time be present to yourself, conscious of the moment.

When you judge another, you are the unconscious tool of forces outside your control, which seek to separate you from the ultimate oneness of existence. No conscious being could take part in such a blindly stupid act.

'Forgive them, Father, for they know not what they do.' These were the famous words of Jesus on the cross, concerning those who had nailed him there. He sees clearly the deceit in the actions of his opponents, and does not applaud it. But such seeing does not turn into the emotion of judgement. Instead, it becomes a reflection on the mitigating circumstances of their ignorance, their lack of wakefulness to their true selves. He asks for them to be forgiven because they are asleep, and

114

clueless as to what they are doing. How can you judge the actions of those who are unconscious?

And so it was that he turned down the chance to condemn, and thereby separate himself from the rest of humanity.

*

Another sign of unconsciousness is our obsession with self-image. We have invented our self, how we imagine ourselves to be. We have this picture of our self, and assume it afresh every morning. It is a daily hallucination, which distorts the truths we allow ourselves to receive, and cripples our relationships with others. Who knows what your self-image is, but whatever shape it takes it is an act of vanity. St Paul called himself the greatest amongst sinners. He couldn't cope with merely being an average, nothing-particularly-special sort of sinner, which would have been more accurate. He had to be the worst! These hallucinations are evil, and paralysing for our development.

The conscious could never have an image of themselves. You might as well try to bottle a waterfall.

Self-image is the creation of our ego and bears no relationship to the truth. If you imagine you are caring, you are wrong; if you imagine yourself moral, you are wrong; if you imagine yourself laid-back, you are wrong; if you imagine yourself wise, you are wrong; if you imagine yourself bad, you are wrong. Whatever you imagine, you are wrong. You are playing a role, not yourself. You are the prisoner of a cramping mental contortion.

You differ from others but only in what you do or don't do – not in what you are.

Your true self, of course, never appears in your mind because it doesn't live in the mind. Its life is elsewhere.

Only when we are present to our true self, our essence, are we conscious; only then are we awake, and alive to spontaneity.

*

Third, we are going to drop the illusion that we are one, a unity, a permanence of will.

Imagine a ship on the big sea. What is surprising is that, although there are many crew members, there is no captain. And the chaos is clear for all to see. Arguments break out between the sailors as one grabs the ship's wheel, pulling it this way, before another wrenches it from him and pulls it the other way. The ship makes uncertain progress as a result.

And that is the human psyche. A chaos of emotions, feelings and thoughts, without a guiding hand.

This is not how we imagine ourselves. We imagine a mature and competent captain at the helm of our ship, with integrity of purpose, consistency of vision. But this is hallucination. It is just the deck hands taking turns at the wheel and they are quite out of control.

All is not lost as long as we bestow no authority on the chaos. Our thoughts, wishes and emotions are not real. They come from nowhere, and return to nowhere. My bad thoughts about you today are one hand at the wheel; my good thoughts about you tomorrow are another hand at the wheel; my sadness yesterday was yet another hand, and my elation tomorrow will be yet another hand still. There are thousands of these characters within us, and if you feel self-pity or irritation at such a possibility, then there are two more of them, yanking at the wheel for their brief moment of influence, each in their turn so convincing that really they must be true, each sounding as though they are definitely the captain: 'This is the captain speaking,' they say.

We will not believe them, however. We will not bestow authority on them. To take them seriously only encourages further lunacy.

'I' do not exist. Only my many 'I's. My self-respect is in tatters at this revelation, but maybe that is a good thing, for that self-respect was a further hallucination. There is no captain on my ship, no guiding hand. Many exist. But 'I' do not exist. That was just an illusion.

Now, finally, I exist.

*

The invitation in this chapter has been to drop our illusions. They have crushed us like weights while we have borne them, heavy with deceit. They will fall lightly to the floor now, for they have no substance, and no existence outside our mind.

And as they drop soundless to the ground, there is no anger in us. Indeed, we are surprisingly grateful to them. For it is through the lie discerned that truth is uncovered. You cannot see beyond the world until you have seen through it. As the Buddhists say, 'If there were no illusions, there would be no enlightenment.' Illusions become our guide out of the forest.

*

If we want to live beyond what life has made us, this letting go is the beginning, middle and end. We must let go in order to receive. To accept the new, we must first put down the old – and the old is everything we ever thought we knew.

The exchange, however, is worth it. For we give up a limited, rather minor belief – a distorted organising of knowledge, overseen by the ego – in order to receive something more spacious, gracious, liberating and hopeful. It is not a new belief system we step into, for

118

all belief systems are redundant. Rather, we step into an open, accurate and lively experience of reality, a clearsightedness boasting eternal views. We stand as one on top of Mount Everest – without actually having to go there.

Though if you get the chance, of course, how fortunate you are.

*

Enough. We were bought from the slave block by the unreal. But now gold has been paid, and we are free.

*Today, as I drop the illusion of control over my own destiny, I am reminded of a dry riverbed, helpless victim of a long and savage drought, brought to life by the rains. The same riverbed that lay parched now flows full, attracting life around it.*

*But don't ask the riverbed to explain how it happened. It just happened.*

# 7

## Prepare for Truth

*Don't seek the truth – just shed your opinions.*

Japanese Zen master

Knowledge is easily passed on. For knowledge is just a sequence of words. It might be complex scientific theory, or a quirky fact on a lollipop stick. Either way, it is just a sequence of words passing on information.

Anyone can pass on knowledge.
No one, however, can pass on understanding.
For unlike knowledge, understanding is not just a
  sequence of words.
Understanding must come from our own work and
  experience.

It is the gradual disentanglement of twisted textures
within us.
Understanding is the slow creation of space for all
things.

*

The house inside was a peeling wreck of dirt and squalor,
but the householder was offered some beautiful gold
curtains, made of the finest silk, and took them. He put
them up in the front room for all to see. They were
most striking curtains – and the word on the street, as
everyone saw them in the big window, was that everything else inside had changed as well. The householder
had changed everything!

This was not so, however. Nothing else had changed.
The house was still damp, still dirty and still overrun
with vermin. The householder had not lifted a finger to
sort things out and, with his marvellous new curtains,
there seemed even less need than before to do so. The
gold curtains on public show were surely change enough.

But because the house didn't change, the curtains did.
The house did not get better, so the curtains got worse.
The damp wrinkled and rotted the fabric, the dust settled
layer by layer, dimming the shine, whilst the vermin
treated it as a brand-new toy, running up and down,
snagging thread with their claws. It was not long before
the once-glorious curtains had been reduced to the level

of the rest of the house. And in time, the householder came to resent the gold curtains. He had had such high hopes of them, but really they had made very little difference at all.

*

If we are not ready to receive great truths in our lives, we will only spoil them as they are incorporated into our shabby inscape. We are like a supermarket with a filthy warehouse. All produce that makes it to the shelves, however fine on arrival at the store, is hopelessly soiled and unusable. In such a state, life's vivid and penetrating truths become tired and faded. We cannot understand them, so we reduce them to something we can grasp – knowledge, information, regulations and rules.

*

How then can truth reach me? What I am seems to be blocking who I might be. I might be seeking truth, but find myself denied it by the very person life has made me.

Confucius would one day become a famous philosopher and moral teacher. But when he was young, he went to Lao-Tsu for wisdom. Lao-Tsu did not have a great deal to say to him, for there isn't a great deal to say, but he did say this: 'Strip yourself of your proud aims and numerous desires, your complacent demeanour and excessive ambitions. They won't do you any good. This is all I have to say to you.'

And with that, Confucius was sent on his way.

The pursuit of truth is not an intellectual affair. It is merely the dismantlement of our attitudes.

To receive truth, I need above all things to create something new inside me, a space not previously developed. I need to create a middle space, or in-between place – somewhere that is other than both my startling essence and my claustrophobic personality. A place where I can take off my coat and simply experience myself. A place to listen for who I am, free from the tyranny of personal agendas. A place where I can begin to trust my experience as something other than my manipulative ego. A place where I could prepare to hear the truth, and perhaps to recognise it when I do. What a fine place that would be, if I could create it: an inner sanctum, a clean space within.

The search for truth is all in the preparation.

*

When it comes to truth, we tend to look in the wrong places. We look for it in inspired utterances, fine music, large buildings, magic words, startling beauty and blinding flashes. We seek it in new experience, travel, the hands of new-born babies, outer space, interesting ideas and flowerpots.

Such things are all very well, and sometimes much more than well, lifting us into a moment of ecstasy if we allow it. But ultimately they are the wrong place to be seeking the truth. They are all gold curtains in their way, vulnerable to who we are within. We assume we will recognise truth, but it is not so. We assume we are open to revelation, but it is not so. We need to assume less, and prepare more.

Imagine planning and saving for years for a trip to the Grand Canyon, only to arrive there and feel nothing. You try desperately to feel what you think you ought to be feeling – but it doesn't happen. Somehow, the whole exercise has a manufactured feel to it. You just assumed the Canyon would do it for you, and the brochures had encouraged you in this. 'Have the experience of a lifetime!'

But you were not prepared within, something the brochures hadn't seen fit to mention. Instead you were noisy, careless, elsewhere, distracted. There was no space for the experience. And so, on arriving home, you could, if pressed, talk of the Canyon. But it hadn't, in truth, been that grand.

*

This moment of discovery and revelation – the one you were hoping for at the Grand Canyon – has been called

124

the mustard-seed moment. It is a moment requiring two simultaneous experiences: the external experience of the thing perceived, and the internal experience that is ready to appreciate it. This is why two people can look at the same view and experience very different reactions. They share the same external experience. But their inner experiences are poles apart.

We see outside us what is inside us.

The great moment, therefore, is not the sight of the flower growing out of the wall by the side of the road, but my *experience* of the flower growing out of the wall by the side of the road. I have walked past it for a year, and not noticed it, but suddenly today I experience its growth as surprising, hopeful and entirely appropriate for me right here, right now. It takes two, however. The mustard-seed moment is an ecstatic collision of two experiences, inner and outer.

*

How we receive our impressions is significant. Impressions are opinion-formers of considerable influence. Impressions determine much consequent attitude and action. So how they are received and formed is crucial. A dirty doormat makes for a dirty home, and negative impressions make for a negative soul.

People don't tend to question their impressions. Most assume that their impressions are true, just as they assume that summer follows spring. They are correct in only one of those assumptions, however.

A pleasing exterior may well accompany a dubious interior, and vice versa.

Most of our impressions of people and events are the stale reaction of our personality, with its fixed and random rules. Our personality can only live in the past. It has no relationship with the present, which means that spontaneity of response is quite beyond it. Our impressions, therefore, do not come to us pristine. They come to us via an intermediary, our personality, which made its mind up about everything a long time ago. This would not necessarily matter but for the fact that everything it decided was wrong.

We trust our personality to deliver our impressions to us, but this is a mistake. It is like relying on a bath-shy chimney sweep to hand you your clean linen. Things will change for the worse in the process of exchange. The linen you receive will not be how it was.

Jesus said, 'Seek the truth and the truth shall make you free.' Unfortunately, your personality is not giving you the truth, and so freedom is not a possibility.

\*

In the eyes of a child, nothing is yet fixed or rigid, and nothing yet a threat. Instead, everything is new, everything is open and everything a possibility. It is not surprising therefore that we are so often encouraged to become as a child. For all psychological and spiritual development is rooted in our ability to take things, hear things and see things in a new way, making fresh connections.

Spirituality is the art of making connections, and when we do, this is a sure sign of our true selves bubbling to the surface.

Our personality will not be making fresh connections. Our personality is determinedly the same as yesterday.

But we are not our personality.

For those who escape personality, time ceases to be. Some people are more alive at eighty than they were at fifteen because the spirit, once released from personality, does not age. It is eternally youthful. The body may be far from youthful, but the spirit is. The body may be tethered, but the spirit is free. In this state, they become today's child, again and again and again, receiving impressions fresh every day.

Fresh bread is better than stale.

*

It is a most wonderful thing to set out in search of the truth, and to follow where it leads, no matter what. In our journey, we will clash initially with our learned conscience – the strange little mish-mash of ideas, whims, and fixations gathered unknowingly from various authority figures in our past. As this was the last psychological layer to form, it will be the first to resist when we make our bid for freedom. It will be very quick to tell you what you can and cannot do. But we will not give it too much oxygen. It is a discredited history teacher to whom we no longer listen.

When we were born, we were a clean slate of possibility. It is possible we do not take the mystery of ourselves seriously enough.

*

The old man had looked after the Old Curiosity Shop for many years. He was the caretaker in a way, because he took care over it. And down the years he had watched people as they stood amazed at his collection of treasures from all times and all places. They would touch them wonderingly, as if allowed into a mystery quite beyond them. Each exhibit must have such a story to tell! Adults acquired children's eyes with the intrigue of it all.

And then, when they had done with looking, they would all ask him the same question. After they had gone round peering at the exhibits, they would turn to the old man and say: 'So which in your opinion is the exhibit in this shop most full of mystery?'

'Me and you,' he would reply.

*

At the heart of the mystery is your essence. It rests wonderful and wild at the heart of your being, untouched by the savagery of life and indestructible against its onslaughts. It remains as it was at the beginning, perfect and unscarred, at the centre of your soul.

Your soul is the adventure of your essence. It is through your soul that your essence engages with life.

It is also through your soul that you lose your way. A lost soul is a soul that has lost touch with its essence, and become trapped in the defensive structures of personality in the battle for survival. We can never lose our essence: it is enduring and eternal. But we can lose sight of it. It can be eclipsed by our obsessions, whatever form they take.

And then, like the visitors to the Old Curiosity Shop, we begin to imagine true mystery to lie not in ourselves but in external things and beyond us.

*

But truth finds us when we let it.

We do not need to strive. Striving does not work.

Neither do we rid ourselves of our ego by pushing it aside in frustration and anger, and straining every sinew towards perfection. As the novelist said, 'Our faults are cured not by will but attention.'[7] It is through simple

---

[7] Iris Murdoch.

attention to our ego that we wear it out, and exhaust it of possibilities. It will fade quietly for lack of opportunity. Truth will fill the gap created.

So we shall not strive for truth, for there is no need. Indeed, it has been said that it is best not to strive for anything, for striving is concerned with goals, and there are no goals, for you are perfect already.

Striving is a tool of the ego, to keep you busy and desperate while you are missing the point.

Instead, the search for truth is a quiet and non-demonstrative business. It's not really a search or a business at all – but an unveiling. It is the fearless and simple exposing of error in ourselves, the ruthless unveiling of motive. And out of this quiet exposure arises a new space within us, in which we can receive new impressions.

We begin to notice things. We begin to notice how we hurt people. We begin to become aware of the negativity that blights our days. We become aware of our endless self-justification. We become aware of the same life lived again and again and again.

And as we notice, and refuse to avert our eyes, what essence we become. We are the bravest of the brave, and the most to be honoured, for the steady refusal to lie to ourselves, or deceive ourselves, is perhaps the noblest human act of all.

*

Patience is a virtue, and one we will need, for the coming of truth is slow, like an elephant's stately progress through the jungle.

Truth cannot come quickly. And by the time we are ready to receive it, we are sometimes barely alive. That is the way that it is. We learn and grow slowly.

How often people will say something like this: 'I would have laughed in your face if you had said that to me two years ago! I see it now, of course, but then? No way.' We recognise a truth, not because it is suddenly true, but because we are ready at last to receive it.

Until then, we laugh in its face.

*

On Monday, the man told me that grass is often green.

I said how ridiculous, and argued my case rather well.

On Tuesday, the man told me that grass is often green.

I said I had occasionally seen green grass, but not to the extent he suggested.

On Wednesday, the man told me that grass is often green.

I can't remember how I replied, though I believe I may have concurred in a general sort of way.

On Thursday, I told the boy that grass is often green.

He said how ridiculous, and argued awhile. I could hardly believe his ignorance.

We can only receive what we are ready to receive.

*

It is quite something to be prepared to be wrong, to be open to your own incompleteness. It prepares the way for truth.

A woman who had experienced emotional breakdown said that she had met the Devil in her visions and she recognised him for who he was because he had such hopeless eyes. She said, 'You know, sin is not smoking too much or drinking too much. It is something that grows inside you and makes you think you are right.'

Seedlings will not flourish in cluttered ground, and new truth will not flourish amidst self-righteous error. Preparing the way for the truth is never wasted time – indeed it is the only essential time, without which all other time is wasted. And then, with the clearing done, we wait and watch, for in a while, as if a spring bulb had been planted, we are rewarded with movement, with fresh shoots of enquiring life.

It is not about being right. Being right is a concern of the ego, but not a concern of the free. Here is fresh energy for existence, and here, within our selves, inner experiences we can trust, because we have neither manipulated them nor imagined them into being.

*Today I am busy with mop, bucket and disinfectant, cleaning and clearing my inner hallway. It's not panic stations. But truth has said she is coming sometime, so I need to clear a space. She's tried before apparently, and found the door wedged shut with clutter. I don't remember it, to be honest – perhaps I was out. She came, pushed at the door, sensed resistance, and left.*

*Not today. It will be different today, whenever or however she comes.*

# 8

## Cease Separation

*Every name from which a truth proceeds
is a name from before the Tower of Babel.
But it has to circulate in the tower.*

Alain Badiou

We are watching a terrible thing.

A young child is frightened and frustrated, and her soul panics. In her shock and fear, she loses touch with her essence. There is a loss of connection. Instead of her soul reaching down into the goodness of her essential nature, it identifies instead with her forming personality, releasing angry energy through her body. She becomes a demon of self-centredness, a terrifying and threatened anguish of screaming 'ME!'. Irrational, fearful and unpleasant, she feels separate from the world and furious. She must be obeyed, she must have her way; her will and desire are the only good cause. All else must bend or break or die.

We are watching a young child become a terror.

In a while, the anguish leaves her, of course, and she is sweet and happy again. She is content with her circumstances – perhaps an arm has been put round her, kind words spoken, or a toy placed in her hands. She returns to her peaceable essence, rooting herself again in its beauty. Once again, she becomes an open, engaging and merging being, purged of separateness and at one with the world.

Until the next time fear strikes.

*

We see clearly how easy it is for the soul to panic and lose relationship with its essence. When the holding hands of life let us slip, in our panic we are prepared to give ourselves to anything if it seems to help. Each time this happens in the life of the child, each time the holding hands of life seem to fail, it will be harder for her to get back to that trust, until one day she won't come back at all.

One day, she will simply not come home, and become a missing person to her true nature, her essence. One day, she will not trust herself again to seemingly helpless goodness. One day, she will so identify with her personality that she will never return, and in time she will forget there was ever anything else.

Now she is separate to the world, and how things have changed. When she was very small, her consciousness contained the world. There was nothing in the world that was not perceived as her. There was no one who was separate to her being, no one who was not a friend. Now the roles are reversed, and the world contains her. Her consciousness is walled and protected. Everyone is separate.

\*

We are standing by a flowing stream, the surface awash with busy bubbles. You call out to them, 'So what are you then?' With some indignation, most of them reply, 'We're bubbles,' and hurry on in a state of haughty offence. But there are other bubbles who do not appear so indignant, and you dare to ask them the same question. 'So what are you then?'

Their reply is as peaceful as that of the others was turbulent. 'We're stream,' they say.

A sense of distinctiveness without a sense of difference is a most skilful attitude to acquire.

\*

Our commitment to our rights and our endless accounting of perceived wrongs is one of the acid tests of separateness. Our separate self is a touchy individual, quick to take offence. 'Do they know who they are talking to?' the separate self demands. The separate self is owed by everyone. Every slight against their person is well remembered and dwelt on with some relish. It may have happened twelve years ago, but it is still fresh today in a stale sort of way.

The vanity is breathtaking. And the sense of separation tragic.

*

One of the problems is our physical body.

There is nothing wrong with the physical body – far from it. The physical body is a miracle of balance and wonder, an organism of mind-boggling complexity and potential, healing and endurance. But it is not who we are. We are not our body. Our body merely hosts our spirit for the time being.

As the baby looks out on the world, it doesn't see its body as the limits of its self. The consciousness of the baby knows no bounds, spilling out all over the place, like an overflowing bath. The infant identifies itself with the wholeness of all things, nothing less. What is more natural? Here is the oneness of all things, spoken of by the mystics down the centuries, and real at the beginning of life.

The child has needs, but believes these will be met, for the world is one with them. Who can be my enemy if everyone in the world is in me already?

But as a sense of abandonment sets in, as we move from essence to personality, as we opt for unreality and illusion, the boundaries of our physical body begin to acquire increasing significance. Like a fence placed round some grass, they seem to define something. The grass becomes a 'field', and you become your 'body'. Neither the field nor your body is ultimately true. The fences will rot, and so will your body, but right now, they look convincing.

The grass is a field, and your body is you.

Such identification is easy to understand. Your body self is the one you dress and look after, and glance at in shop windows as you pass. It is your showcase at the party, your hallmark as you walk. It's the body you use to compete with others in any number of ways. It is always with you, every day, and stands in for you in public, when you want to remain hidden within; it is the daily means by which people judge you. It requires a lot of attention, certainly, but can give a great amount of pleasure also. It is in the photos when people say, 'There you are!'

No wonder we identify with our bodies, and begin to imagine them to be our precisely bordered selves.

Yet my body has actually got very little to do with me. I look after it, because I live in it. I run every morning to exercise my heart and sweat out my anger. But my body is not who I am. For my real self is fluid space – unattached, merging, pure, spilling, and infinite, as indeed I once knew myself, before experience exploited my vulnerability and suggested otherwise.

To confuse your physical body with your self is a recipe for misery. For though our bodies are miracles, they are ageing, faltering, fragile, collapsing, vulnerable, disintegrating miracles. To ally ourselves with them is as wise as leaping on to a bus as it heads towards the cliff edge. Our physical bodies are not the future, and therefore they cannot be our present either. They are not us. We live with them as best we can, and for some that is a good deal easier than for others. But we never imagine that they define us or contain us.

*

Once we become bordered people, once non-separate becomes separate, once the illusion is launched, it spreads like wildfire. The insanity is duplicated, multiplied, replicated in all sorts of ways, at many different levels. We separate into genders. We separate into colours. We separate into social classes. We separate into sporting rivalries. We separate into sexual preference. We separate by age. We separate by culture. We separate by geography. We separate by religion. We separate by politics. We become cut off from each other, as those in the Tower of Babel, and strangers to truth.

We like our tribes, we like the negativity they permit, we like the way they damage the oneness of all things.

We like it how it is: some people in, some people out. Otherwise how could we pass judgement on others?

Separate selves are kings of categories, and queens of division. It's the only way to organise things, bring order to things, rationalise things. Some versions of this game may be harmless enough. If the nursery teacher asks all the boys to go and stand in the sea corner, and the girls to gather in the home corner, there is no great evil being done. But ultimately those children are not two groups but one group.

In the adult world, the separation of one group from another has had rather more serious repercussions.

Evil has only one cause, and it is neither Satan, nor upbringing, nor genes. It is simply the notion of the separate self, the soul seeing itself as a discrete entity, strong in its sense of centre, a particular and bordered kingdom.

If you do not realise that you and I are one, there is no limit to the terror and pain you will unleash against me when you feel the holding hands of life let you slip. You become the terror of self-centredness, a threatened anguish, a screaming 'ME!'. Irrational, fearful and manip-ulative, you are separate from the world and furious. You must be obeyed, you must have your way – your will and desire are the only good cause. All else must bend or break or die.

*

Our personality must always be at the centre of its universe. It is too insecure in its rigid and fixed ways to be anything or anywhere else. From this place, it can enact compassion, but it cannot *be* compassionate. It can do compassionate things, but these must be deliberate acts of worthy striving, knowingly done, and applauded by the ego.

If we live from our essence, however, the universe itself becomes the centre, and we become part of that. From this place, identifying with others comes quite naturally and unknowingly. We feel at one with others, and this is true compassion. Compassion is then not something we do to be kind – it is just our being.

And so it is that the great religious leaders have not attempted to change society. They have not been social reformers. Rather, they have sought to reform the chemistry of the human condition. They have been less concerned with making social programmes and more concerned with making social people – people able to think, feel and act as sane people, at home to their truest selves, and at one with the world.

*

Once we come home to the world, we stop segregating others, and become suspicious of labels.

We see, for instance, that there are no weak people and no strong people. There are just people, sometimes weak and sometimes strong. 'Weak' and 'strong' are just labels, and all labels are lazy. A person who sits weeping and weak with me one day may very well be strong the next day in another situation. While I, strong for her on that occasion, feel weak the day after. So who is strong and who is weak?

Strong at lunchtime, weak by supper. This is how we are. Not strong people or weak people, but sometimes one and sometimes the other.

People are laid low by different things. Physical illness, mental illness, emotional traumas, and spiritual darkness; short-term crises and long-term difficulties; people are tired, stressed by work or simply under-valuing themselves. But we will not pigeon-hole them as weak. For despite their weakness, each possesses great strength. And sometimes it's *because* of their weakness they possess great strength.

Weakness is part of who they are. But not all of who they are.

So there are no caring people or cared-for people. There are just people. Sometimes caring, sometimes cared-for.

We know how weak people can be. We know the effects of Alzheimer's. We know the vulnerability of a tiny baby. We know the devastation of brain damage and physical disability. But as soon as we separate and declare someone weak, we deny them the possibility of mediating strength, and therefore deny them their humanity.

The weakness may be overpowering. But it's only part of who they are.

Some people may not help themselves. Some demand their separation. Some for instance will insist on being strong all the time, adopting the role of the one who looks after others. And some will insist on being weak all the time, declaring themselves a constant mess, and always in need of help.

But we will sit light to all such separation, and all such labels. These are not skilful attitudes, and we do bad things to people when we separate them from ourselves.

*

We are on a beach, and there is the king surrounded by his loyal retainers. It is King Canute shouting against the incoming waves, ordering the tide to turn round and retreat. His retainers stand expectant. The waves must surely turn back if the King commands it? The King is God's anointed one, and separate from the rest!

But they were to be disappointed. The point of Canute's lunacy was to show his retainers that kings were very much like them, that the waves would no more obey him than they would the third spear-carrier from the left.

It was a tough illusion to crack. The word on the muddy street was that kings were different. This was the common assumption of the times. But as the waves advanced, lapping playfully and insolently around the throne, blissfully uncaring of the fact that this was God's anointed one, Canute's point was made. And behind the throne, as the chill water seeped into the loyal retainers' sandals, the shocking message was reaching the wider community. The King was not separate.

Nature doesn't recognise our distinctions because they do not exist. Every category dreamt up, every differentiation made, every distinction drawn, every exclusion enacted is a further step from the truth, a vain shout in the face of reality. We build careful and deliberate sandcastles of division and separation – but the only reality is the sea of unity. It is the ignorant who imagine that their thrones and sandcastles will survive beyond the evening tide.

\*

Imagine a figure of salt suspended above a beautiful ocean. The salt figure is going mad at his experience of separation, and yet clinging to it. 'Who am I? Who am I?' he keeps asking, without being able to answer the question, for he has no understanding outside himself. Yet something or someone inside him keeps on asking, 'Who am I? Who am I?' and slowly he realises that he is descending towards the water. He panics, for this will be the death of him. The water will absorb him; he won't be the famous salt figure any more with his trademark looks and poses. He screams as his feet touch the glorious depths. He can feel his feet slowly dissolving, and then gradually the rest of his body. He is losing his lovely edges! Now he will never know who he was!

Yet, as the last bits of him break off and merge with the water, a sudden sense of peace comes over him, a sense of becoming part of something he had chosen thus far to ignore. And as he finally and completely joins the ocean, the last words of the salt figure are these: 'Now at last I know who I am.'

As a seventeenth-century writer said, 'You never enjoy the world aright, til the sea itself floweth through your veins, til you are clothed with the heavens, and crowned with the stars.'[8]

Our imagined distance from creation fades to nothing, and we experience the truth that 'the true being of separate beings is non-separate being'.

*Today, I am spilling out of my body, for I am the world, and my body is too small a container. You might as well ask a thimble to contain an ocean.*

[8] Thomas Traherne.

# 9

## Know Your Soul

*Art is something which, although produced by human hands, is not created by those hands alone, but wells up from a deeper source in our souls.*

Van Gogh

You have travelled overnight, arriving in the dark, too weary to notice anything, and now as you wake you have no idea what to expect. You have heard so many different opinions about this city, some saying it's the best, and others dismissive of it. As for you, you just wanted to see for yourself, so you could make up your own mind.

Gradually, as your dreams fade, you become conscious of where you are. You adjust your position in the large hotel bed, as the morning light filters through the curtains of your room high up on the twelfth floor. It is time to see things for yourself. You walk across to the window, your sleepy eyes glad of the gentle half-light and shadow. The curtains are thick, but you grasp them well, and pull them open with a flourish. Suddenly unbelievable light is filling your room, light you had no inkling of before! Your eyes are blinded by the brilliance, but desiring also to see as your face feels the sun's warm rays even at this early hour of the day.

Your room is invaded by the morning light, and beyond you, below you and before you is a city basking: a city aglow. You cannot take it all in – this is a world in itself – but the architecture, the vistas, the smells – you have never seen anything like it.

You drove through it last night, but in the dark you saw nothing, and in your exhaustion looked for nothing. Now, however, it is different. Now it is as if you are seeing it for the very first time. And you can't wait to explore.

It is a delight to become acquainted with our soul. Our soul is the very stuff of our life, the material and texture from which our life emerges and is comprised. When we react to a comment made, reflect on a situation, decide to overtake the car in front, or paint a picture of a sunflower, our soul is our operational centre – the place from which these acts arise.

Our soul is everything – mediating between our personality and our essence, and part of both. We need to know our soul like the virtuoso cellist knows her cello.

The cellist knows every inch of her instrument's possibility, every weakness in its structure, every strength in its design, every nuance of its sound, every resonance in its body, and every delight to be had from its being.

She knows and loves the instrument with which she works – and so it is that the music unfolds from within.

*

It is hard to overemphasise the importance of the soul. It is at once our window on reality and our experience of reality. The soul holds all our inner events – visual, theoretical, emotional, visceral – making us aware of them, and creating our response to them. It receives the event, interprets the event and acts in response to the event.

Our soul is our entire experience. Our soul *is* our world. If you have a big soul, you have a big world. If you have a small soul, you have a small world. It is possible to have a soul bigger than this planet. It is also possible to have a soul barely larger than a pea. No two human souls are the same, for each reflects the intentions and dispositions of its carrier.

The nature of our soul depends on that where it is planted. As a flower planted in good soil flourishes, so does our soul rooted in our essence. A soul rooted in our personality, however, will be a stunted and struggling creation.

Liberation of the soul is the dissolving of fixedness and rigidity, insisted on by insecure personality.

Liberation of the soul is the tender and deep collusion with our essence.

The soul is not a given, therefore, served up in one size only, the same for all. It is a creation with endless variation of shape and nature, which starts with a desire in your mind, and can become anything. The adventure of the soul will not stay in your mind or end in your mind, but that is where it will start, in a desire to explore and a wish to uncover.

If the thought to discover becomes desire, and desire becomes will, then the soul journey has begun.

*

You may not get much initial encouragement in this quest. Indeed, there might even be some embarrassment on your part. On the shop floor, outside the school gates, and at the golf club, talk of the soul is generally considered inappropriate, and rather intense.

The materialist cannot believe in its existence. They must see it as the sad invention of religion, unscientific and unnecessary for the explanation of anything. The human merely takes in impressions and excretes behaviour. What place is there for a soul in this process?

The religious, on the other hand, tend to domesticate the soul, imagining it to be a slightly precious place within, designed to contain our more spiritual feelings. The soul is presented as a port in a storm amidst the tempests of harsh life. It is a resting place for the weary pilgrim.

However, we will not follow either of these paths here. Rather, when we use the word soul, we use it to describe a cascading waterfall of experience, all power and fluidity, all change and force, all energy and life, a crashing vastness of possibility and engaged at every level of our physical and psychological well-being.

In common parlance, 'The person has soul,' is a comment about the depth, courage and compassion in an individual. Common parlance here is on the way towards the truth.

But of course every person has soul. It is not the particular possession of a favoured few.

*

The moment we realise that we are not a machine is also probably the moment in which we cease to be one.

Some people talk of the human body as a machine, and in some respects it is. There are clear principles on which it runs, specific needs to keep all the working parts in order and functioning as a unit.

But the human body is hardly a conventional machine.

It is a machine that can self-harm, for instance. There is not a cell in our body unrelated to our emotional state.

Our physical body is part of our subconscious, and emotional pains held in our body become stubborn and stuck, stopping the flow of life through our cells.

Medicine cannot always help people who are held captive by emotional experiences retained within.

It is also a machine inhabited by spirit. How often do we see an elderly couple follow each other closely in death? Once one has gone, the spirit is weakened in the other and the machine closes down. Physical death is not just about the physical body.

*

And so, quietly, the soul presses its case, inviting us to realise. Rumours of essence percolate through us, until one day we step outside, look up at the changing cloud formations in the sky, and dare to declare to ourselves, 'I am not a machine.' We may not yet know who we are, but this does not matter.

At least we know what we are not. And this is a very big moment.

*

Until this moment, there is undoubtedly a machine-like inevitability to our lives. We are asleep to ourselves or unconscious, machines comprising little more than a series of programmed responses from our past.

The human machine in this state cannot manage genuine spontaneity, or genuine freedom in the moment. Nor can it grow. It can function for years in well-established tasks, achieve many things, sometimes to great applause and appreciation, but it cannot grow.

Circumstances may change, but human machines don't. They perform as programmed, and to the extent and variety of response allowed by their programme. The human machine does not know the programmer. It just relentlessly lives out its will. The human machine is the same at eighty as it was at thirty, though obviously there is serious physical wear and tear. The machine will run as long as the battery lasts, and do as well as the setting allows. But that will be it. That will be as good as it gets.

So it is really a very good day when we realise that we are not a machine. Change is not sudden, for our formation was slow and many-layered. Each layer must now be visited on our return journey.

But it is now another world. We are learning how not to be a machine. We are beginning to root our soul in our essence, and hear it speak new things.

*

The madman, on day release from hospital, was once shown round an undertaker's. He was a little odd, but most interested in all that they did. Downstairs, they had a coffin-making department. He was left alone there for a while, and decided to fill the time by lying down in one. A little like Goldilocks, he made three attempts before he found one the right size, for coffins play hosts to many different shapes.

Once he found it, however, he discovered that a coffin is a good place to be whilst still breathing. Pressed on all sides by the wooden walls of death, he began a most lively conversation about life. He lay in the coffin laughing, thinking of lots of mad things he would like to do before he died. He also thought of regrets he did not want to have when his time on earth was done.

On discovering the madman in the coffin, the shocked undertaker rang for the hospital to come and get him immediately. 'He has flipped,' he told them. 'He's in a coffin, laughing.'

The madman had not flipped. Indeed, he had just touched on sanity, allowing himself to be educated by death, allowing death to guide his life. The undertaker couldn't understand, however, and shaking his head in bewilderment at this morbid nutcase, rang the hospital, before returning to the land of the sane upstairs, where shocked and grief-stricken clients were waiting. You would never find them laughing in coffins! God forbid! They took death rather more seriously.

*

Often death is shocking precisely because we have not been mad enough in life to allow the coffin to speak. People live in denial of death, because it is not considered to have anything to say – nothing cheerful, anyway. So when death comes, it is shock, and grief and confusion, and a sudden rush to find meaning.

Little that is good emerges from this cycle of denial and rush.

The coffin educates us for life – not for death.

This is the territory of the soul. These are things our soul can receive, consider and act on now. Our personality cannot handle such things. It would prefer to ignore. But such things are food and drink to our soul.

\*

A story of two men one Monday morning:

The man left his small flat to walk down the busy road to work. He could get a bus but, if he left home twenty minutes earlier, walking was fine, particularly on a morning like this, and it saved the fare. He had lived alone in the flat since the collapse of his marriage, and had found it hard to get work due to his lung condition. But now he was the cleaner for a care home run by the Social Services, and he was happy there. Early start, but early finish too, except on Thursdays when they had the bingo after lunch. He'd wanted to write a book called *Life After Everything*, because there was, but a publisher told him there was no chance of a deal, due to his lack of profile. It may be good stuff, but who would be interested? He'd accepted this, but been aware of a sadness within himself.

This morning, however, he could see red tints in the sky, feel the tell-tale chill of early September, and smell the arrival of autumn. It was just magic.

At exactly the same time on exactly the same day, the President kissed his wife on the cheek, and was driven from his large apartments to the presidential gym, where he would work out for half an hour, before going to his office. Today he would receive world leaders, gathering to assess the economic stability of the West. He was happy today as he was high in the polls, and unchallenged in power. Due to retire in two years' time, he already had a book deal for his memoirs running into millions, and a lecture tour set up, which would almost equal that. His publisher knew people would buy his book without thinking, and attend his lectures as a matter of course. As an ex-president, he would clearly have something to say of significance and substance.

The President himself could not have told you what

the weather was doing this particular morning. It was just Monday.

One of these men was human. One of them was a machine. One lived from his inner space. One lived from his programmed path. The world would pay big money to hear from the machine. They would pay nothing to hear from the human.

*

As we have noted, the soul can become identified with the conditioned shape of personality and physical body. The soul can falsely assume itself to be trapped and separate, like a free bird imagining itself in a cage.

But there is another way. As gradually we cease to identify with our conditioning, we unimagine the cage, and go free. We realise that our soul is this ever-changing entity, fluid in form, shape and size. Sometimes our soul breaks its banks, bursts forth and spills out way beyond our physical body. At other times, it is something shrivelled, tight, and considerably smaller than our physical body, like a peppercorn knocking around in a large trunk.

The nature of our soul depends completely on its relationship with our essence, where our true colours lie. Rooted in the indestructible beauty of our essence, the soul will feel big, almost to the point of being able to put its arms around the world, in easy generosity. Rooted in such perfection, the human soul is a substance without frontiers, a city aglow, welcoming all.

But if an emotion like fear is able to distract the soul from its true colours; if a mental message of danger and fright is able to triumph over essence, then the soul can wither very quickly, and become a pinched and cramped container with room for nothing except hate towards that which is making it scared.

We remember watching the child become a terror. As soon as the child felt the holding hands fail in some way, the child's soul panicked. It shrivelled in fear, and separated into selfish and terrified tantrum.

Common parlance would not suggest that this person has soul. Just look at their behaviour! But they do have soul. They have a magnificent soul. It is just that it is presently in the wrong hands.

*

Another big moment in our lives is discovering that we are our own happiness.

For happiness is neither an emotion nor a reaction, but a space – a space within us. If we want to consider happiness then we must consider space.

True happiness is a space within us where all experiences and feelings can be received. This strong inner cavern can receive and hold the raw energy of any emotion our personality throws at us, whether it is disappointment, elation, guilt, sadness, jealousy or rage. The personality is a torrent of various and shifting energies. Yet this space within is never waterlogged by emotions, for it is distinct from them, with its own prior identity.

The space is permanent, the emotions passing.
We live the space. We do not live the emotions.

It is important that this space can receive all energies in an unthreatened manner. It does not accept some and reject others. It notices, receives and accepts all. Rejected energies are dangerous to our happiness, as they tend to lodge within us, causing blockages in our being, effecting every level of health.

But where there is space in the human soul all energies can be received and acknowledged. Once noticed and received, whatever their nature, they will cause us no ill and may bring good. Negative energies will disperse harmlessly, while beautiful energies will percolate vibrantly through every fibre of our being.

Removed from the cramped roller-coaster of emotional indulgence, we live a spacious contentment.

All serious spiritual and psychological work will be towards the creation of this space within us, for it is the creation of happiness.

*

We can enjoy our jobs. We can enjoy mountain climbing. We can enjoy our children. We can enjoy amateur dramatics, buying jewellery, playing Scrabble, surfing the Internet, going on holiday, or being Prime Minister. We can even enjoy our charitable works. But these activities in themselves do not constitute our happiness. We alone are our happiness.

Coming home to this truth, however, is a difficult journey. It is understandable that daily we turn back from it, and seek happiness in places external to ourselves.

There are those who trace the roots of this issue back to the child on the mother's breast. There, in the earliest days of formation, the child learnt that all true nourishment came from *external* sources. Happiness and security was established as something to be sought in the world beyond. And this simple untruth is never quite unlearned.

It is an untruth because there is no world out there beyond our soul. Our soul receives the world, interprets the world, and acts in the world. If we do not start from our soul, our within, then we are starting from an illusion, which will deliver only sporadic and brief contentment, and a tedious cycle of pleasure one day, pain the next.

This is how it is. The dog leaps delighted when food time arrives and sulks five minutes later because food time is over. And the mother is delighted when her child shows affection, and so hurt when the child doesn't respond as she should. And the carpet salesman hates

Saturdays because of the pressure in the shop, loves Saturday nights, because he can walk out of the shop and go straight to the pub, hates Sunday mornings because he has a head like thunder. We feel reassured when someone is alive, and we don't know what to do with our sorrow when they die.

The roller-coaster of duality demands that what gives pleasure later gives pain, and we accept this as the normal inner human experience. We call it the rich tapestry of life, though it generally isn't very rich at all. We have stopped expecting anything else, imagining that beggars cannot be choosers. We will take what we can get, and what we can get is out there, and external to ourselves.

But true happiness is within. It is the space emerging from our essence.

\*

I remember a woman made hard by sadness. She was emotionally and physically cold, locked in the past. She was taking part in a visualisation exercise. She was initially disconcerted and frightened. She found herself walking in her imagination through a long dark tunnel, which offered her no relief. This was a state she was familiar with.

But she was not familiar with what happened next. Suddenly she was standing in a place brilliantly bright, colourful and warm, vast and vivid. It could hardly be more different from the tunnel, which had seemed endless.

She had never imagined within herself a space such as this. It had been there all the time, but its possibility had never been spoken of by others.

It was only a glimpse, and she has since lost sight of it often. Her struggle will always be to live from that colourful place, and not the cold and unforgiving tunnel.

It is a struggle that starts afresh each day.

*

To be present to the soul is to know ourselves greater than our thoughts, feelings, images, moods and understanding. At the heart of our soul is our unimaginable essence. Beyond our worries, goals and cravings, all seeking redress or satisfaction in the external world, lies the mystery place within us, where all things are perfect, exactly as they are.

The treadmill remains an option, if that is our wish, but we will not pretend that it leads anywhere. It just goes round and round and round. It picks you up, and it dumps you down. People sometimes say they want to get off, and then something comes up, and they never quite do. But don't imagine that it is the only option.

*

You are the beggar sitting on the box by the side of the road, as you have done for years. You are eking out a living, arms outstretched, and calling to passers-by. You need them to survive. You have always needed them. A coin or two, that was all – and then you would be happy for a while. If they gave more, then that was a very good day.

There's a woman approaching now, and you ask her for money. She turns you down. But she not only turns you down. She tells you to look in your box. You tell her to mind her own business, that you've been sitting on it for years, thank you very much, and have no need to look inside it. You call out to another passer-by. Surely they will give you something?

But the woman won't be distracted. Again she is telling you to look in the box on which you sit, on which you have *always* sat, and which has become part of you. You know that it is a meaningless exercise to look, but with no one else to call out to, you go along with her, hoping she will move on, and stop wasting your time. You have always had the box beneath you, though who knows where it came from? You have never looked inside it, but then why would you? This is madness. As if anything of value could be there! You think you might just have noticed, after all these years!

Still, you humour her for want of a better idea.

You open the box to find solid chunks of gold. Your begging days are over.

\*

*Today, I contemplate the vast and impressive space that is the international airport. I note the planes arriving every two minutes from a multitude of locations. I watch the many planes departing to lands beyond. And I am thinking of my soul. Endless. Receiving. Sending.*

# 10

## Fear Nothing

*When you lie down, you will not be afraid; when you lie down, your sleep will be sweet.*

The Book of Proverbs

There was a monk who pestered Buddha about the finer points of philosophy. He felt that Buddha had the answers, and with more knowledge all would be revealed. Clearly he couldn't make any commitments yet. But when he knew everything, then he would. Then he would start the journey.

But Buddha rudely told him he was like a man wounded in battle, who refused treatment for himself until he knew the full name of the person who had injured him, and the village they came from. He would die before he got his useless information. 'Do not fear to live the teaching just because you do not know all the answers yet,' he told the monk.

And we might go further. Do not fear to live, full stop, for we cannot 'live' in fear. Fear is an illusion and there can be no life in illusion. Life is allowing the unfolding, and in such submission there is no one who can hurt you.

*

We are not concerned in this book with what you can do for others, because you cannot do anything for others – except defeat your own fears. If you were to defeat your own fears, then you could help others. If you could defeat your fears, then you would suddenly be a living fire of possibility, which others would gather around, drawn to the warmth amid their cold.

But we do not embark on the spiritual journey for the sake of others. If the perceived requirements of others are our primary concern, there is a distortion in the process, ensuring our journey becomes an exercise in deceit or vanity.

The deceitful wish to save others because they fear facing themselves; they prefer instead the comforting applause of the admiring world. They are like the ill, who are determined to share their disease with others. All they have to pass on is their fear.

We, however, face our fear for no other reason than

that we ourselves would like to be free, and to live a beautiful life. And without fear, experience is almost unbearably beautiful.

As Jesus said, seek first the Kingdom of God and all other things shall be added unto you. As Jesus also said, the Kingdom of God is within.

*

Fear arises in our enslaving imaginations. It does not exist as a separate entity out there that bangs on our door and forces its way in. Rather, we both create it and host it. Fear is our own creation, but one that grows into a monster. Feeding on past experiences in our lives, fear towers over us like a huge and darkening wave, waiting to break, waiting to smash and crash, waiting to fall and engulf us.

Our lives are crippled by the gnawing feeling of fear. It is hard to be free from it. Cut off from our essence, where all things are perfect, we become susceptible to wild imaginings of our destruction.

*

We express fear in different ways, for we fear different things.

It is not unknown for those who achieve some success in the world, and acquire a following, to declare themselves 'bigger than Jesus Christ'. This is how they express their fear, for what they fear is their annihilation. One way of handling the fear of death is to seek false consolation in hallucinations concerning your own status.

But the fear of death creates other responses. See the person, for instance, who lives the moral life to gain the good opinion of others. Here is someone equally fearful. They too are motivated by the ultimate fear of annihilation, but deal with it differently. With no peaceful answer to their future death, how they are perceived by others now becomes intolerably important. They need the validation of being seen to be doing the right thing, as consolation and massage for their self-love. When people admire them, they are flattered and cheerful. When people blame them, they are depressed and angry. So they make New Year resolutions to do more for others; they try to remember to ask after the health of others in order to appear caring, and they run a marathon to raise a very public £2,000 for charity, but more importantly, to be perceived as someone who puts others first.

In the face of the black hole at the heart of their existence, they seek the admiring applause of others to ease the psychic pain. Take away their reputation, and they have nothing.

No wonder they will drive themselves to distraction in good works. Cut off from their essence, they do not trust existence. Lacking internal validation of their own, they crave the external validation of others. They do not trust their inner perfection, so they choose to live from the only alternative place to trust – the place of fear.

\*

Jason was fifteen months old, and had enjoyed the baby room in his nursery, where he had been a happy child. But recently, things had changed. The arrival of five new babies, all younger than him, had meant that the adults were suddenly busy with needs other than his own, and could not hold Jason as and when he liked. This was the end of the world for Jason, and he screamed a lot, in sheer despair. But he also began to find a solution – for he discovered that if he wandered into the next-door room, the older children fussed over him, and there was always a spare adult's lap. So this he would do, until he was stopped from doing it. Then he screamed even more. His clever solution was being frustrated by bad and nasty people.

One of the nursery teachers tried to reassure him. She said that she was busy with Gemma at the moment, but as soon as Gemma was settled she'd be with Jason, and they would read his favourite story together if he liked. But he didn't like – for Jason, that was not sufficient. He wanted to be held now, right now, like he used to be, and so he screamed and screamed and screamed.

How could he know how safe and cared for he

actually was? Everything inside him told him something different. But everything inside him lied.

Like Jason, we do not trust life. And so fearfully we try and force things with our own solutions.

*

Nothing can harm our essence. It is indestructible, and therefore we are indestructible. We can easily become cut off from our selves. We can become stranded like beachcombers in the caves at full tide, our paths back home cut off, flooded by the waters of fearful imaginings.

But the tide will recede, and so will our fears, for they have no substance. They have no eternal existence; they are reaction, the mere panic of a soul cut off from its roots.

*

Sometimes it is the social institutions we inhabit that create fear. Governments create fear of torture. A mortgage creates fear of non-payment. Others' expectations create fear of failure. Religions create fear of judgement and hell. Companies create fear of redundancy. Groups, tribes, faiths and gangs create fear of difference. Magazines create fear of fatness. Nosy neighbours create fears of being watched and talked about.

Social institutions have no authority in themselves. Authority is something bestowed, always our decision, and the courage to stand alone has often been the mark of a hero. Our heroes swim fearlessly against the tide, and refuse to bow to convention. But they are few and far between because most lack the necessary core of peaceful certainty.

We fear that if we offend social expectation, we die.
But such fear shows only that we died a long time
  ago.
Died to our courageous selves.

*

We fear deaths, small and large. We fear the death of being found out. We fear the death of slowly losing our mind. We fear the death of missing our big chance. We fear the death of a loved one. We fear the death of the missed bus. We fear the death of other people's judgements. We fear the death of inner emptiness. We fear the death of the unsuccessful interview. We fear the death of physical pain. We fear the death of feeling hopeless and abandoned. We fear the death of plans not working out. We fear the death of rejection. We fear the death of a collapsing relationship. We fear the death of things not being as they should be. We fear the death of failure to achieve. We fear the death of our cat stretched out and limp in the road. We fear the death of everything falling apart. We fear the death of passing time, lost time, wasted time. We fear the death of experiencing ourselves as we truly are. We fear the death of being bad parents.

We fear all things, instead of living all things. We fear all things, while all things are perfect.

There is nothing to fear – except staying as we are.

*

A man is running along a quiet country road. Three miles before breakfast, and then on with the day. Suddenly, from out of the undergrowth, a frenzy of activity. A pheasant is panicked by his approach, and squawking, leaps out in front of him, running ahead, fearing itself chased and hunted. It is driven mad by fear, as this huge presence behind it bears down with thumping speed.

For a hundred yards, the runner follows the pheasant, scuttling its terrified way along the road before it turns blindly into the hedgerow and calm.

The man runs on, laughing at the stupid pheasant, so frightened about nothing. What did the pheasant have to fear? The man meant the pheasant no harm. The fear was all in the mad creature's head, an illusion.

But how can a pheasant not fear, when fear is all it knows?

It can be equally hard for humans.

*

We will not imagine this a war easily won. Each battle with fear is a battle against layer upon layer of childhood learning in the art of survival. The first part of the human brain to develop beyond the womb is that which deals with fear, anger and satisfaction. When we were at our most vulnerable, it was fear that alerted us to perceived danger. It was fear that encouraged us to contort ourselves in order to survive.

In the hidden history of our past, we lived a thousand fears, and composed a thousand schemes in response to those fears. Those schemes became our very texture.

Fear was important. We are alive now because we
    are fearful people.
But what helped us then does not help us now.
Fear is a foundational part of our personality.
But it is not presently an energy for our development.
Your essence knows no fears because, unlike your
    personality, it is unscarred by life. It remains
    hopeful, vibrant and strong.

*

And here lies the truth beneath the mystics' claims that all is well in the world and that all is just as it should be. For beneath the lacerating distortions of life lies the perfect world in each human soul, and the truest identity of each. There is nowhere else to go, for you are there already.

Fourteenth-century England was dominated by war, famine and plague. It was not a good century in which to be alive. But after twenty years reflecting on a vision given to her, an English hermit of those times wrote down these words: 'All shall be well, and all shall be well, and all manner of things shall be well.'[9]

The kingdom of heaven is within, and all within is quite perfect, which is why when we lie down we will not be afraid, and our sleep will be sweet.

*Today, I walk in safety across the battlefield. I may be hit – but I won't be hurt. The bullet is busy, but I am at peace. In fact, I would throw it back if I could be bothered.*

[9] Julian of Norwich.

# REPRISE

*There is a tide in the affairs of men*
*Which, taken at the flood, leads on to fortune;*
*Omitted, all the voyage of their life*
*Is bound in shallows and miseries.*
*On such a full sea are we now afloat,*
*And we must take the current when it serves,*
*Or lose our ventures.*

William Shakespeare

When swimming in a cold sea, it is most wonderful suddenly to feel a warm current enveloping your body. Perhaps you hadn't realised how chill you were until this gentle heat touched you. You are not sure where it is coming from, and suddenly it is gone, lost as quickly as it was found. It disappears into the depths, and only the cold is real again. It is colder still for your recent experience of the warmth.

Then your foot again finds the warm, elusive but there, felt and experienced. One leg and then the other leg is touched. And slowly you begin to understand the nature

177

of the warmth in the cold sea. Sensing its origin and flow, you find you are able to hold yourself for longer in its grasp.

Our essence is the warm current in the cold sea. We are happy indeed if we learn to hold ourselves there.

## SOME CLOSING THOUGHTS

It is a sobering thought that life does not develop people, that experience of life in itself does not make for growth.

Think of a seed. A seed is a self-developing organism, but will stay as a seed for a million years unless the conditions for growth are right. The seed is full of potential, but will change not one jot until placed in soil and fed with food, air and light. Life does not develop the seed. It could knock around in a thousand different and interesting settings and not develop at all. It would be experienced in life, but not in the least developed. It would remain unlived potential.

And so it is with humans. Life does not develop us if it is not the right sort of life. The idea that we are learning, evolving, changing and growing as we go is a sad nonsense. What some people call 'experience' is, more accurately, a rut of non-redemptive pattern, not twenty years of experience, but one year's experience lived twenty times. And there is a thin line between a rut and a grave.

The human being is no more the finished article than the acorn. In order to become an oak, the acorn will need to be planted and rooted in something other than itself. It may mean the end of that nice shiny shell, but that was never meant to be more than temporary. Like the acorn, a human being is just a beginning with a long journey ahead.

What is made of the journey varies a great deal, and it is our capacity to develop skilful attitudes to life that determines the shape of things. It is with these skilful attitudes we have been concerned here. Certainly we are not all on the same level of development. All may be of equal worth, but we are not equally aware. Some make a great deal of the human journey, and some almost nothing at all. Some take the tide at the flood, others lose their ventures.

And of course we speak here of the inner journey, and look with the inner eye. Witness the unpleasant nurse, and the kind bookmaker. Labels mean nothing in the real world.

*

To say that all humans are on the same level of development is on a par with saying that all piano players are on the same level, from the child of four banging the notes with his chocolate-covered fingers, to the silky-fingered, emotionally focused concert-hall maestro. There is excellence in music and there is excellence in human existence.

*

We are not all on a level of development, and most are adult only in the number of years they have physically lived. We can have travelled the world, led armies in battle, brought up a family of eleven, and greatly advanced medical science, without for one moment having had to step out of our bankrupt personalities. We have engaged with the world, but not necessarily with ourselves. We are those who have looked for growth in experience, like the seed trying a thousand different settings. So much experience! But it is still a seed. If we imagine growth is automatic from experience, we might as well look for fish in a tree.

Yet the strong word on the street remains. In libraries, railway stations and shops; in mosques, churches, temples and synagogues; in yoga classes, hospitals, and motorway service stations; in boardrooms, brothels, government buildings and restaurant kitchens the world over, there seems little doubt – we are children no longer, adults now and on a level. We know what's what. We have come of age!

The truth could hardly be more different. The truth, strangely, is that we actually know less than we did as a child. We have not come of age. We have acquired much, but lost everything. We are a shell of the person we were at our beginning.

*

So what does a beautiful life look like?

It doesn't matter where we meet it – it will always look and feel the same. It could be in a car mechanic, a tulip importer or a banker; it could be in a teacher, a barman or an artist. Their role is irrelevant. It is the work beneath the work that creates the beautiful life, and its characteristics are always recognisable, before even a word is said.

To meet a beautiful life is to meet a spacious and gracious presence, open to all people, available for all things, yet holding on to none. Fluid in spirit, they will be as happy on the territory of others as they are on their own.

They will know clean truth – truth that is the fresh fruit of daring curiosity and clear seeing.

They will display an emotional spontaneity, wholly present to the circumstances, yet free of desire to manipulate or control.

They will possess pure will, flowing easily from sweet places within, a deep and strong river of inner guidance.

They will be aware of their purpose, place and function.

They will live from their being, rather than from the opinion of others.

They will live from trust, rather than fear.

And their hand on heart will be their hand on their solar plexus.

The beautiful life will have no agenda but the best possible present for all.

They will have no home in themselves but the adventure of unfolding creation, and no energy within but that inspired by thankfulness and wonder.

The beautiful life will let go in order to receive, receive in order to cherish, and cherish in order to understand.

Such people laugh because they can see, and love because they can do no other.

They are those who have moved from confusion to identity, from action to presence, from separation to communion, and from exploitation to contemplation.

They are, in short, a seed set and nurtured in the soil of their own perfection.

*

To this extent, no one can teach you anything about being human. Your essence itself knows already all there is to know. It understands and already *is*, more than anyone can speak of. Already, in your potential, you surpass the wise sayings of any guru, enlightened one, or prophet. These people can startle, provoke or point you *towards* your essence, but they must then back away, and shade their eyes – for your essence outshines them.

*

We will be practical people who do what is necessary in life.

I will happily clean the company toilets, for these things must be done. But I will not identify with the company, just as I will not identify with the charity I give to, the youth club I help at, the circle of family and friends I have, the dream I harbour, the feelings I experience, or the god I worship.

There are some things that should be beneath everybody.

I will cherish – but I will not nurture attachments.

183

*

You are lying in a hot bath, amid steam and foam. There is no striving to be contemplated in a place such as this. You just relax and enjoy.

So it is with the ten skilful attitudes outlined in this book.

Everything is work, but not everything is striving. There are no checklists to make, boxes to tick, failures to be punished, or self-recrimination to be indulged in. There is just the thought that if we pay attention to the familiar there might be a life beyond our habitual ways, and this thought gives birth to the journey – a journey we probably started long ago.

And the rewards of the journey are fine. For seeing a new humanity arise in you out of the old has been compared to seeing a sword being drawn from its scabbard. The scabbard is a similar shape and one thing, but the sword is something else altogether.

They can scarcely be compared.

*

And so we return to where we started, and the figure of fire. The woman in her dream was a figure of fire, alive and burning bright. Slowly, however, and against her will, an encrusting mass began to grow around her, choking her into unconsciousness and leaving her for dead . . .

Time passed. The fire figure lay enclosed in the airless dark, suffocated by the thick crust around her. There was no way out. In her chill dying, she remembered faintly what she had once been, but was too weak now to imagine any going back.

The enveloping substance was overpowering and final, permitting only itself.

Yet as she dared to remember what had once been, she sensed strange change. For, as she remembered, her cold bones spawned wisps of random flame, dancing surprisingly into life from her body – weak flickers at first, but each encouraging another, and then another still.

The airless dark, once the ally of the crust, began instead to aid the fire, becoming a conduit of heat and light to the imprisoning lava.

And soon, fractured by the heat, the first crack appeared in the crust, after which there appeared another. The fire figure breathed new air, responding with fresh burning. Purple and red, green and blue, yellow and orange, the fire figure found again her truest and most brilliant colours.

In the face of such heat, the lava crust splintered and cracked in disintegration. It was a good coming home.

Light will some day split you open

Even if your life is now a cage.

For a divine seed, the crown of destiny,

Is hidden and sown on an ancient fertile plain,

You hold the title to.

Hafiz

A NOTE ON THE AUTHOR

Simon Parke has written satire for radio and TV, picking up a Sony Radio Award. He was a priest in the Church of England for twenty years but now works in a supermarket, where he is Chair of the shop Union. He leads retreats, strives for the beautiful life and lives in London.

# A NOTE ON THE TYPE

# A NOTE ON THE TYPE

The text of this book is set in Berling roman. A
modern face designed by K. E. Forsberg between
1951–58. In spite of its youth it does carry the
characteristics of an old face. The serifs are inclined
and blunt, and the g has a straight ear.